The Golden Days
of San Simeon

"Pleasure is worth what you can afford to pay for it."

William Randolph Hearst (1863–1951)

The Golden Days of San Simeon

By KEN MURRAY

Foreword by Ronald Reagan

GOVERNOR, STATE OF CALIFORNIA

Garden City, New York

DOUBLEDAY & COMPANY, INC.

For the three girls in my life,
BETTE LOU, PAM, and JANIE

Format and typography by Joseph P. Ascherl

Contents

Foreword

How does one write even a foreword for this journey into a period and place so touched with the golden haze of nostalgia as to be almost unreal?

Yes, I know San Simeon, but only as a story or rather a collection of stories—all fascinating, all true. When I first came to Hollywood, as a very green and overawed sports announcer supposed to become an actor, I listened on the set to the tales of weekends at San Simeon told and topped by stars, directors, and other assorted greats of movieland.

At the same time or thereabouts, I met a man who knew firsthand the glamorous life of San Simeon, Ken Murray. We have been friends for many years. Lately Ken has become a specialist in Hollywood folklore. His home movies are the most unique chronicle of the history of Hollywood.

It is like him to share this chronicle with the millions of people who may visit the Castle at San Simeon. For the first time in history, visitors to a castle will see movies of the man who built it, living there and entertaining his famous friends. And the visitors will be in Mr. Hearst's private theatre as they view that chapter of his life.

Now, as a member of the California State Park Foundation Board, Ken has written this commemorative book, bringing the golden days of San Simeon to life with never-before published pictures. He takes us from the turning of the first spadeful of dirt on the Enchanted Hill through the glittering time when San Simeon was the exclusive rendezvous of the most famous people in the world to a tour of the Castle as you see it today.

Others have researched and written about San Simeon, but Ken Murray was there, a part of the cast of characters, and he generously shares this experience with all of us. We are in his debt.

RONALD REAGAN

Governor, State of California

Preface

This book was written on the fiftieth anniversary of the building of San Simeon, 1919–69, and to this day no one knows exactly how much Mr. Hearst spent on the Enchanted Hill. A rough estimate, including construction costs, improvements, land and gardens and art acquisitions, is in the neighborhood of fifty million dollars.

Contemplating what possibly could have induced a man of our time in democratic America to indulge in such unheard-of extravagance, one of Hearst's excellent biographers, John Tebbel, wrote: "Plenty of American millionaires had more money than Hearst, and most of them handled what they had with more wisdom, but none enjoyed his wealth as much. That was because of Hearst's attitude toward money. He did not regard it as invested capital or as an industrial resource. He thought of it with charming simplicity as something to spend."

Maybe what the writer called simplicity was much more than that. Considering that in reality the temptation to spend money for things we want and don't really need is something that everyone can understand and identify with, and considering the uncertainties of life, perhaps Mr. Hearst, in enjoying his wealth, displayed a real kind of wisdom.

Mr. Hearst made millions and he spent millions; not how he made his fortune but how he spent it and shared it with his friends is the subject of this book.

For the privilege of enjoying the hospitality of this most gracious host, I trust Mr. Hearst will emerge from these pages a human being, exhibiting the private side of his character that only a few ever saw.

If so, I hope the experience will become warm and personal and exciting for each reader of this book.

KEN MURRAY

1 - William Randolph Hearst, the Builder

William Randolph Hearst was the most unusual and unique public figure that America has ever produced . . . and San Simeon is the most spectacular private residence ever imagined by a human being. Kings live in palaces they inherit, but this man built a castle that was the ultimate in earthly magnificence, inside and out.

San Simeon, constructed from several castles shipped over in crates from Europe, represents twenty-eight years of labor and an investment of untold millions of dollars. It has thirty-eight bedrooms, fourteen sitting rooms, thirty-one bathrooms, two libraries, a kitchen, a billiard room, a movie theatre, an Assembly Hall, and Refectory (dining hall). In addition, it has three guesthouses—La Casa del Mar, La Casa del Monte, and La Casa del Sol. A total of 146 rooms in all. Within the Castle there is also the beautiful indoor Roman swimming pool, little used, probably, because of the magnificent 104-foot outdoor Neptune Pool, surrounded by formal gardens filled with Greek and Roman statues.

The building of San Simeon was extremely difficult and expensive because it was not planned functionally from the start. It seemed to grow in an endless mosaic style to suit the housing needs of Mr. Hearst's vast collections of art objects and to satisfy his memories of decorative arrangements he had seen in the castles and cathedrals of Europe which he wanted to duplicate in his own palace. One simply cannot conceive of the extent of his antique acquisitions. In Eastern and Western warehouses were stored entire Gothic rooms, paneling, carved ceilings, staircases, stained glass, mantels, choir stalls, columns, tapestries, and countless other things that would stagger the imagination. He wanted all of it incorporated into San Simeon, and so it became not only a gigantic

George Hearst made a fortune in mining and accumulated vast land holdings in California and Mexico.

building project but an extremely complicated work of assemblage—a magnificent fifty-million-dollar repository for his memories and collections, undoubtedly the most costly and unusual private residence ever erected for an uncrowned mortal. But Mr. Hearst always refused to call it a castle—to him it was always "the ranch."

What contradictory qualities were in this man that caused him to construct the most magnificent personal dwelling place in the history of mankind and then give it the plainest of names?

Some of the answers may lie in his background, his childhood, his growing up. An only child, he was born in San Francisco, April 29, 1863, into a grand style of living, but there must have been something unchangeably democratic and honest at the core of this man's personality. His life was the opposite of the Horatio Alger story. His father, Senator George Hearst, was one of the richest of the early Western mining tycoons. His mother, Phoebe Apperson Hearst, was a woman of excellent taste, culture, and artistic perception. And together they saw to it that William—or "Will," or "Sonny," as they called him—had every kind of educational advantage.

It was his father who gave him the love of the outdoors.

George Hearst, born in 1820, the son of a Missouri farmer, was an amiable, well-liked man, and extremely generous with money. The things he enjoyed most were work, politics, pioneering, gambling, animals, and of course, his wife and boy. His son, William, loved him, and inherited his sense of humor, his grandiose manner with money, and the trenchant way he regarded the world. George Hearst's mining interests kept him away from home a great deal. He was known as one of the best judges of mines in the world and the demands on his time were great—he once received $50,000 for a single consultation. The times young William spent with his father were infrequent but enjoyable, and W.R. recalled later that he always remembered him constantly coming and going with valises full of quartz specimens.

It was his mother who gave him the love of the beautiful things in the art world.

Phoebe Apperson Hearst, born in Missouri in 1842, was a petite woman, with enormous gray-blue eyes, grace, charm, and a sense of humor. Her life revolved around three major interests: her son, art, and philanthropy. It was she who supervised and guided her son's life. She

Phoebe Apperson Hearst and her first two grandchildren, George and William Randolph, Jr.

felt him to be a superior child and pampered him, praised him, indulged him, and sought always to enhance perfection. He adored her—he idolized her—and she unstintingly enveloped him with a love that was overly maternalistic and that had an affect on all his adult relationships with women. At a very early age she began to instill in him a love of the arts. Her husband, twenty-two years her senior, although overly generous in giving her anything she had a desire for, was not culturally oriented, and so, while he was pursuing his business and political ventures,

William Randolph Hearst—
"Willie"—about the time of his
first trip to Europe with his
mother that established his
lifelong mania for collecting.

she embarked on a program of absorbing everything she possibly could
to enrich herself of these things and was determined that they would
be a part of her son's life.

Carefully planning the trip for some time, in 1873, when her husband
would be gone for nearly a year, she and William Randolph, aged ten,
left on their first excursion to Europe. They visited England, Scotland,
and the Continent, and it was on this trip that her son's enthusiasm for
the arts was crystallized and he pursued it for the rest of his life.

Around 1874, W.R.'s father went on to the biggest strike of his career—the Anaconda mine in Montana, which soon was producing one fifth of the world's supply of copper, besides several million dollars in gold and silver.

In 1887, the Hearst family had two momentous happenings. William Randolph Hearst, then twenty-four years old, took charge of the San Francisco *Examiner*, owned by his father, and began a career which was to become journalistic history. The same day George Hearst became a United States Senator and started serving his first full term in Washington, D.C.

The Senator took his position very seriously. He was a conscientious worker and was well respected by his colleagues. Phoebe became one of Washington's most celebrated hostesses, and gained a reputation for being an extremely generous and benevolent woman. A little-known fact is that Phoebe Apperson Hearst, while in Washington, was responsible for saving Mount Vernon from ruin and restoring the original furniture.

With his fine business acumen, George Hearst was continually buying huge real estate tracks all over the West. Perhaps the most significant of these was his purchase of the forty-thousand-acre Piedras Blancas ranch in central California, which ran from the San Simeon Bay on the Pacific Ocean back through the Santa Lucia Mountains. It cost him seventy cents an acre.

Originally the ranch was called "Camp Hill." George Hearst used it for picnicking with his wife and young son, William.

When W.R. had acquired a family of his own it continued to be a camping place, an ideal spot to "rough it" with his growing sons. However, these sojourns began to take on an elaborateness that was a forerunner for things to come on the Enchanted Hill. It was even laid out in the same manner as the future San Simeon. There was a huge circus-size main tent, and around it three smaller guest tents, each one divided into four rooms and a bath. There was also the bivouacs pitched by the servants and chauffeurs, the tutors and nurses, and the whole site gave the appearance of a small, early Western town. As in the latter days on "the Hill," paper napkins were used, and all the condiments, jams and jellies, etc., were put on an old oaken dining table in their "store" containers. And it was in those early days that the nightly rite of the cinema

From the beginning, he had his eye on a commanding hill nestling in the craggy Santa Lucia Mountains, with a spectacular view of the Pacific Ocean.

began. Long before San Simeon was built, Mr. Hearst was projecting crude flickering pictures on a sheet inside of the big tent.

Hearst loved California more than any place on earth and the rugged ranch at San Simeon drew him like a magnet. He never had any doubt that some day, when time and money permitted, he would build a castle on this escarpment atop the imposing Santa Lucia Mountains.

At that time, "Camp Hill" was almost a wilderness, rising two thousand feet above the Pacific, but as his future home was being carved out of this rocky mountain top, Hearst renamed it La Cuesta Encantada, "The Enchanted Hill," which is what it gradually became.

Mr. Hearst visited San Simeon many times during the construction and the hardships of building there were endless. Clearing the 123 acres at the crest of the hill was a Herculean task. Mr. Hearst loved trees and could not bear to see a big tree cut down. It cost thousands to move

A road was built at great expense up the mountainside. Steel and cement began arriving by coastal steamer.

Unwilling to see any tree cut down, Hearst ordered this giant oak moved in a huge container of concrete, estimated to weigh more than 600 tons.

Julia Morgan, one of the first women to practice architecture, was classically trained and perfectly attuned to Hearst's grandiose dreams, and her engineering skill made them a reality.

each of the giant oaks that were in the way of construction. The crew of workers, always numbering between 25 and 150, not only battled weather, but tarantulas and rattlesnakes, and the gigantic problem of hauling building material up the mountainside from the bay.

Entrusted with the architecture was a diminutive lady of outstanding professional ability. Julia Morgan was a remarkable woman. Born in 1872, she was raised in a proper Victorian-like manner, and was a brilliant student at the University of California. When she was contemplating her major at that institution, she considered medicine, music, and art, but decided on architecture. The university at that time did not offer a School of Architecture, and so she was graduated from their School of Engineering in 1894, and it was generally acknowledged that this background figured in her later successes. She also became the first woman ever to earn an architectural degree from Paris' École de Beaux Arts.

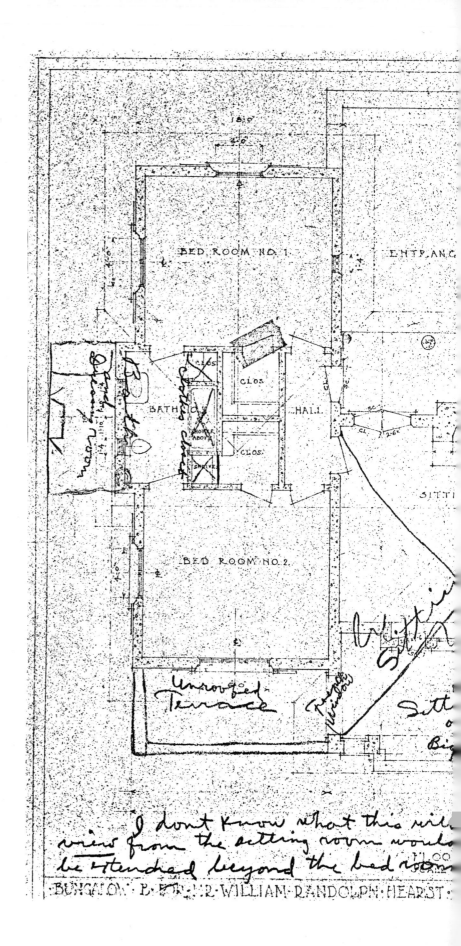

I dont know what this will ~
view from the setting room would ~
be extended beyond the bed room

BUNGALOW B FOR MR WILLIAM RANDOLPH HEARST

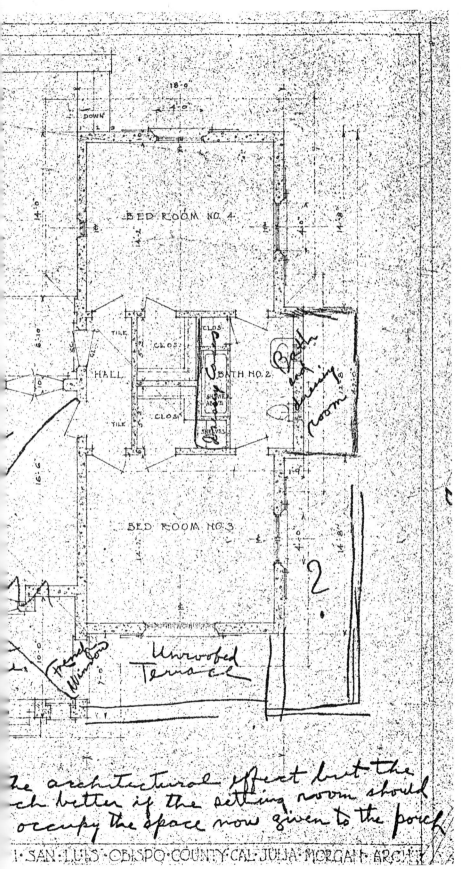

Hearst thought nothing of scribbling his ideas across Miss Morgan's exquisite working drawings. Here he is concerned about the view from one of the guesthouses.

According to her niece, Flora D. North, in an article written for Kappa Alpha Theta in 1967, "Upon her return to California in 1901, she worked for a short period with John Galen Howard, who at that time was the University of California architect and had the commission to build the Hearst Memorial Mining Building, a gift of Phoebe Apperson Hearst. Miss Morgan's work so impressed Mrs. Hearst that she asked her to open her own offices so that she could do work on her own. In time she met Mrs. Hearst's son, William Randolph Hearst, who confided his dreams of building at San Simeon a 'living museum' properly to house his growing collection of art treasures. Unfortunately, he said, no one had been able to figure out how to get the necessary materials to this then remote area. Again Julia Morgan's engineering skill came to her aid. She suggested building a wharf at San Simeon and bringing in the materials by boat.

"In later discussions Mr. Hearst realized that her Sorbonne background of large scale 'institutional' and elegant building was completely suited to his grandiose plans. His tastes were catholic, and he would acquire a Gothic ceiling for which he needed a setting, along with some Etruscan urns and Greek statuary. It was a challenge to mix and use these things tastefully. Mr. Hearst's admiration for Julia Morgan's ability constantly grew, and through several decades and many, many building projects, each enjoyed the exhilaration of working with the other's extraordinarily able mind."

Miss Morgan started working with Hearst on San Simeon in 1919. She was forty-seven years old—Mr. Hearst fifty-six. The scope and complexity of the undertaking required many consultations. Sketches were drawn and redrawn, and each step in the development of the whole was discussed, the decisions being reached only after the most careful consideration. At the height of the building activity there she had sixteen architects working for her.

Although the development of San Simeon involved a very heavy professional commitment and attention to Hearst's definite ideas of design and decoration, Miss Morgan also maintained a very active practice, specializing in educational buildings, hospitals, and churches. Hearst was undoubtedly a demanding client but the working relationship was excellent as revealed in Miss Morgan's own words:

"Mr. Hearst and I are fellow architects. He supplies vision, critical judgment. I give technical knowledge and building experience. He loves architecturing. If he had chosen that career he would have been a great architect. San Simeon *is* Mr. Hearst."

It is significant that the year his mother died William Randolph Hearst started building San Simeon. It seems almost as if W.R. was continuing his beloved mother's lifelong quest for beauty and elegance, and it was Julia Morgan more than anyone else who guided into artistic and engineering reality the childhood dream W.R. was realizing with his energy and his millions.

Finished first were the three guesthouses—La Casa del Mar, "The House of the Sea"; La Casa del Monte, "The House of the Mountains"; and La Casa del Sol, "The House of the Sun"—1919, 1920, 1921. Four years later Mr. Hearst moved into the main castle, "La Casa Grande."

The staggering immensity of La Casa Grande becomes apparent in this view of the early stages of construction. The reinforced concrete shell should last for several thousand years.

Slowly a paradise of horticulture rose on La Cuesta Encantada—the Enchanted Hill—where in earlier years the Hearst family camped and picnicked.

However, it was *not* finished and, in fact, never would be. Hearst had developed what J. P. Marquand described as an "edifice complex." He was a frustrated architect, gripped by a compulsion to build, and it seemed impossible for him to stop. In time San Simeon took precedence over every other activity, and Hearst would continue to add to it for the rest of his life.

The landscaping on the Enchanted Hill—breath-taking in its magnificence and monumental in its cost—seemed to reflect Mr. Hearst's passionate love for beauty, which his mother instilled in him and carefully nurtured through his childhood. In fact, all the gardens at San Simeon were envisioned and laid out by a portrait painter, Orrin Peck, who had been a protégé of Phoebe Hearst.

To oversee this blossoming magnitude, Mr. Hearst hired Nigel Keep, a horticultural expert from England. Starting in 1919, he spent his entire life working at San Simeon. The rugged Mr. Keep presided over twenty permanent gardeners, and always seemed to keep abreast of W.R.'s whims and fancies.

W. R. Hearst and a devoted
friend, Nigel Keep, his
botanical expert. Hired in
1919, Keep spent his entire
life working at San Simeon.

For one thing, all the gardening at San Simeon was done at night, because Mr. Hearst could not abide to have a dead flower on a bush and he did not like to have servants or workmen around him. So, if one stayed up late, or would be awakened in the night, which was very seldom, he would see the gardeners working with torchlights, going around picking off dead flowers and doing silent work in the garden.

One Easter, Mr. Keep, knowing it would please Mr. Hearst, worked with his large crew all through the night by floodlights so that the next morning, Easter Sunday, the Castle, with a touch of mystical magic, was entirely surrounded by tall white Madonna lilies. The surprise of it, the utter loveliness, filled his guests with amazement and Mr. Hearst with pleasure and delight at the thoughtfulness of Nigel Keep.

Opposite above: The Celestial Suite taking shape in July of 1924. This fourth floor apartment, consisting of two octagonal bedrooms with a sitting room, commanded a sweeping view of the Pacific on one side and the Santa Lucias on the other. Later two towers were built on top of the suite, each containing eighteen carillon bells played from a keyboard off the Game Room.

Opposite below: Even before La Casa Grande was ready for occupancy Hearst plunged himself into another architectural orgy, the building of a new recreation wing. Julia Morgan's genius in fitting priceless medieval stonework into a modern shell can be seen at left.

In 1924, Hearst started his animal collecting with a herd of pure white fallow deer imported from Asia. At its peak, his collection rivaled that of many world-famous zoos.

Getting the Castle ready for occupancy involved a flurry of last-minute preparations.

Rare photos showing successive versions of the Neptune Pool. Hearst ordered it enlarged twice before its scale satisfied him, making it unquestionably the most expensive private pool ever built.

In mid-1923, Mr. Hearst became dissatisfied with the size of the original marble-lined swimming pool. He felt it was too small for San Simeon. When advised by the contractor that the pool was a big one as it was, Mr. Hearst replied, "I think it will look better larger, and it will give work to unemployed men." When he was further reminded by Nigel Keep that the kind of a swimming pool he envisioned would cost close to a million dollars, Hearst merely shrugged and lifted his shaggy eyebrows. The pool was enlarged.

Actually, Mr. Hearst enlarged the pool twice. Even when he was ready to move into the Castle—1925—the beautiful marble colonnades from Italy had still not been uncrated and put into place around the Neptune Pool. In addition, the Celestial Suite was not completed and workmen were still moving statues into the Castle. But on Christmas Day 1925, Mr. Hearst and his family occupied La Casa Grande for the first time.

On December 25, 1925, the Hearst family moved into La Casa Grande. The beautiful long refectory table was set with magnificent antique silver and Blue Willow china, but no tablecloth and the napkins were paper. Down the middle of this highly polished table and service stood an army of catsup bottles and pickle jars with the labels on. That's the way Mr. Hearst wanted it—"ranch style."

Christmas had always been a festive occasion in the Hearst household. From the time of his first son's birth in 1904, W.R. delighted in impersonating Santa Claus—a joy he repeated for years to come. He tried to sustain his boys' faith in the saint as long as possible and abhorred anyone who broke it. When they finally realized that there was no such real person, he held them to the thought of the "spirit of Christmas."

And with the prodigality of their father it would have been understandable if the boys never stopped believing in Santa Claus.

The first Christmas at San Simeon was perhaps one of the most exciting ever for the Hearst family. There were two extra Christmas trees set up in honor of Hearst's twin sons, and the Chief once again turned himself into jolly old St. Nick.

2-A Weekend on the Enchanted Hill

In the golden days of the thirties, if you were a member of the motion picture colony, not necessarily a star, the place to spend a weekend was San Simeon—*if* you could get an invitation.

You would be one of the exceptions in the cinema capital if you did not experience a slight thrill of anticipation when the phone rang and a voice at the other end of the line (an Ella Williams, the social secretary) graciously inquired: "If you are free this weekend, Mr. Hearst would like to invite you to be his guest at San Simeon."

Hastily accepting, you were further informed that the private train leaves Glendale station at 7:35 P.M. and will arrive at San Luis Obispo at midnight. There, Mr. Hearst has arranged for a fleet of limousines to meet the party and be driven to the Castle. Your tickets will be at the station and, of course, all expenses will be paid until you return Sunday night. Then she added sweetly, you are not permitted to bring any personal servants—valets or maids—and, naturally, no chauffeurs.

Among the big crowd boarding the private train are the usual Hollywood figures, famous stars of the sporting world, a smattering of Hearst's own employees, and, as always, some faces not quite identified. But the predominance of handsome Hollywood stars such as Clark Gable, Dick Powell, Lew Ayres, Joel McCrea, Cary Grant, Charles Farrell, John Gilbert, and Gary Cooper makes it less like a departure to a private party than a movie junket to a gala première of a big motion picture in some far-off city.

You overhear Hedda Hopper telling someone that they're lucky to be included this weekend, as there are special goings on at San Simeon. A fabulous party to celebrate Mr. Hearst's seventieth birthday. It's going to be a big old-fashioned '49er costume party, and "Don't worry, the costumes are being trucked up to San Simeon from Metro-Goldwyn-Mayer Studio, complete with sewing women, hairdressers, wigmakers, and make-up artists."

In addition to the train contingency, there is a planeload of guests being flown in Mr. Hearst's new big Fokker plane from the Burbank airport to the private field at San Simeon for the festivities. Passengers on this daredevil jaunt will include movie moguls such as Louis B. Mayer, Irving Thalberg and his wife, Norma Shearer, Jack Warner, Darryl Zanuck, Doug Fairbanks, Mary Pickford, Charlie Chaplin, Louella Parsons, the Harold Lloyds, and youthful millionaire producer Howard Hughes, who has just made the sensational box-office hit *Hell's Angels*. Mr. Hearst's close friend A. P. Giannini, founder of America's largest bank, is coming down from San Francisco; Mayor Jimmy Walker is flying in from New York City; Charles Lindbergh will also be a guest with his wife, Anne. There's even a rumor that George Bernard Shaw, who is currently visiting the United States, will attend—however, this seems incredible, as this would make it his only overnight stop in any private residence in America.

The train trip up the Pacific coast is a festive one. When you finally elbow your way into the club car, you find that Mr. Hearst has provided not only plenty of refreshments, but a group of musicians to while away the miles.

Surprisingly enough, among these stellar Hollywood luminaries, the center of attention is the indefatigable Hedda Hopper, completely captivating her audience of beautiful Hollywood people with Hearstian stories.

"This is a little different mode of transportation than when we went to San Simeon in the twenties. In those days you weren't exactly forbidden to drive your own car, but Mr. Hearst preferred that you and all the other weekend guests assemble at a designated time at the Ambassador Hotel in Los Angeles where everyone was assigned to a chauffeured limousine, and then you'd all be driven up the coast in a long line, one after the other, to the Castle. My God! at times it reminded me of a bridal or funeral procession!"

Amid the laughter, she continues: "I've been up to San Simeon so many times that Mr. Hearst says I know every nook and corner nearly as well as he does. The last time I was there Bernie Baruch was visiting for the first time. The Chief elected me to guide him around. At one point we were surveying the view of the Pacific and I said, 'All the ocean front you see—fifty miles of it—Mr. Hearst owns. All that land and those mountains as far as the eye can see, all that except that one tiny peak. The one you can hardly see—' And then, just behind me, I hear this high squeaky voice saying: 'You're wrong, Hedda, I own that peak, too.'"

If it's a surprise that Hedda gets away with these facetious remarks about the host, it's understandable. At that moment, this is not Hedda Hopper, the powerful newspaperwoman that she was to become; this is Hedda Hopper, the actress, not even a star, only a featured player in support of the big shots. She is the mean woman who makes the stars look good. She has just recently been let out of her M-G-M contract and is looking for work.

It would be a couple of years before her friend Cissie Patterson would prevail upon her to write a column for the New York *Daily News*. It would be an instant success. Ultimately she would have an audience that would exceed twenty-three million readers, and though she became the main competitor of Hearst's powerful columnist, Louella Parsons, she remained one of Mr. Hearst's closest friends and was a constant visitor at San Simeon. The explanation for this unlikely friendship is that Hedda Hopper was one of Mr. Hearst's lifelong friends, an association that went back to his pioneer movie days in New York, where Hedda worked in practically all of his Cosmopolitan pictures. W.R.'s friendship, given frugally, lasted a lifetime, and guests at San Simeon were not selected for their prestige, wealth, or their current success, but because they were likable and diverting.

The disembarkment of the large party from the train that arrived promptly at midnight at San Luis Obispo is expedited in typical Hearstian style, and at what seems like no time at all the long motorcade is on its way to San Simeon. Hearst, the eternal showman, has had the floodlights turned on the Castle so that all the arriving celebs can see the twin towers from miles away on the coastal highway. You're informed upon inquiry that the ranch is on 265,000 acres of land and it has an ocean front of over fifty miles. You can tell immediately when you reach the Hearst property, because you turn off a country road that is wild and unkept and then suddenly you are on the Hearst property, which is manicured like a fine hand.

From the large entrance gate to La Casa Grande it is a five-mile drive, and you become immediately aware of Mr. Hearst's tenderness toward animals when you drive up the mountainside, as you are confronted by large signs admonishing all vehicles to ALWAYS DRIVE SLOWLY—ANIMALS HAVE THE RIGHT-OF-WAY.

You're further informed by your driver that the San Simeon zoo and game preserve is the largest private collection in the world, protected from the guests by an eight-foot-high wire fence, ten miles long, sealed by electrically operated gates. It's difficult to remember that you're still in America as the bright glare of the car's headlights reveal sacred deer from India, warring yak from Tibet, llamas from Peru, camels from Arabia, giraffes from Africa, and fighting emu from Australia. You learn further that there are only three natives of North America roaming the Enchanted Hill, the bison, elk, and mountain sheep.

When progress is impeded by one stage-struck water buffalo from India refusing to get out of the spotlight, you are reminded that Winston Churchill had the same experience on his first trip to San Simeon, being delayed on this same private road for over an hour by a stubborn, inquisitive giraffe, refusing to budge.

As the road winds slowly to the peak of the rugged Santa Lucias you are enveloped in a fog of low-hanging clouds drifting in from the Pacific, when suddenly you emerge through the murkiness and see the illuminated La Casa Grande looming over you like a fairy-tale illustration, surpassing even the best of Disney.

Ascending the magnificent outdoor marble stairway, flanked by a profusion of flowers and blossoming shrubs, you find yourself on the main terrace with its quatrefoil-shaped fish pond and the marble statue of Galatea, "queen of the water nymphs," reclining on a dolphin and looking toward the main entrance of the Castle.

Inside, in the center of the large Assembly Hall, surrounded by treasures of paintings, sculpture, and architecture, stands the Chief, one of the most powerful, influential, and controversial personalities in American life, a giant who had been stripped of privacy and dissected like a laboratory specimen by critics all over the world. Despite the

Weekend guests usually arrived at midnight Friday after a festive train ride up from Los Angeles. They found the Enchanted Hill ablaze with floodlights.

By night the ponds and statuary were beautifully lighted by glowing globes of alabaster.

Celebrities followed this tiled promenade to their rooms in the guesthouses.

Making informal movies delighted Hearst and his guests, and nearly everyone visiting San Simeon was photographed. Left to right from the top: the host and Charles Lindbergh; Mayor Jimmy Walker of New York; Hedda Hopper with A. P. Giannini, head of the Bank of America; Robert Montgomery; Douglas Fairbanks, Jr., and Joan Crawford; Claire Windsor and Dolores del Rio.

excitement that always attends arrivals and the distractions of the wonders of the Castle, it is impossible to keep your eyes off the host, who seems to be shyly greeting his guests in a manner less like the "Lord of San Simeon," than a mild-mannered caretaker who is rather embarrassed by his employer's fabulous display of wealth.

Seen at close quarters, across the width of a handshake, the personality of William Randolph Hearst is a staggering surprise, contradicting nearly every preconceived idea that had been formed of his life. He is an impressive man, over six feet tall, who obviously has spent many of his early years in the health-giving life of the open air. His face is large and strong. In repose it is intensely serious; in conversation it is lit up by a smile of extraordinary winsomeness and even charm.

But at this moment he is listening more than talking, and listening as though he were grateful that he has been permitted to attend. When he speaks in his high-pitched voice to graciously welcome his guests, you have the feeling he is going out of his way to put newcomers and unknowns at their ease. It is hard to reconcile this attitude emanating from this powerful man whose very name in the late twenties and thirties could induce terrified chills in so many hearts. But on the top of the Enchanted Hill it is "Hearst the Host"—proud of San Simeon and eager for his guests to enjoy it to the full.

Marion Davies and Charles Chaplin; Arthur Lake; Cary Grant; Claire Windsor and Buddy Rogers; Dick Powell; Carmen and Lloyd Pantages with starlet, Jane Peters, later known as Carole Lombard.

33

Beautiful Greta Garbo is surrounded by a typical weekend's Hollywood notables. Back row, left to right: King Vidor, Beatrice Lillie, Richard Barthelmess, Eleanor Boardman. Middle row standing: Frank Orsatti, E. B. Hatrick, Edmund Goulding, Ma Talmadge, Greta Garbo, Nick Schenck, Alice Terry, Harry Rapf, Aileen Pringle, J. Robert Rubin, Norma Shearer. Seated: Hal Roach, Natalie Talmadge, Eddie Mannix, Constance Talmadge, Buster Keaton, Paul Bern, Irving Thalberg. Reclining: John Gilbert.

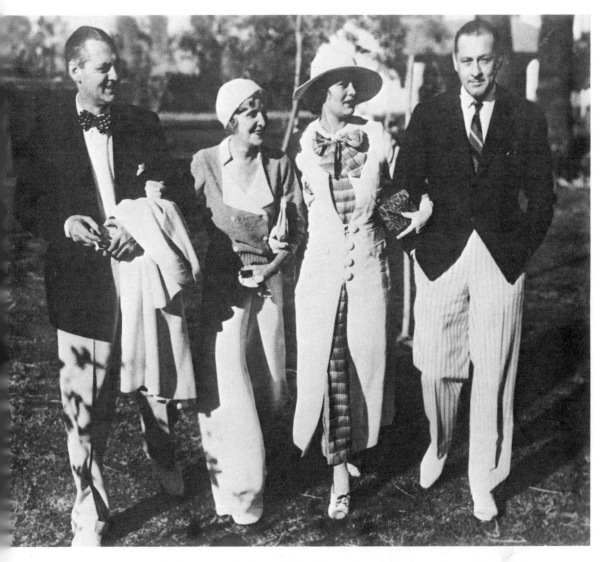

Enjoying a stroll through San Simeon's ample grounds are Mr. and Mrs. Lionel Barrymore and John Barrymore and his wife (Dolores Costello).

World-famed Irish dramatist and Socialist George Bernard Shaw chatting with Marion Davies. Shaw, after viewing San Simeon, is rumored to have said, "This is probably the way God would have done it if He had had the money."

Having arrived at night, first-time guests were up early the following morning to explore the legendary Hill. Stepping out of the guesthouses, this is what they saw.

Long after Mr. Hearst has retired to his magnificent Gothic Suite atop the Castle, and you are comfortably stretched out in your antique bed in one of the beautiful guesthouses, staring at the baroque ceiling from which seraphs and cherubs smile down at you, and listening to the roar of lions and the snarl of panthers caged in the nearby zoo, it is impossible to repress wonderment at the power of this man, who in this one estate controlled an area half the size of the state of Rhode Island. Your mind is still spinning over his unbelievable accomplishments.

William Randolph Hearst, millionaire and extravagant collector of art, a giant of journalism and master politician. Once a member of Congress, he spent millions to be President and other millions to make Presidents. When not running for political office himself, he was right in the thick of other major campaigns, and W.R. had close, personal relations with Wilson, Harding, Coolidge, Hoover, and Franklin D. Roosevelt, whose nomination it's no exaggeration to say he was responsible for securing.

But at this period he had weathered and surmounted the problems, personal and public, of the past, and the future ones, financial and physical, of the late thirties and forties were not even to be imagined. These were the choice years to be enjoyed and savored. At this moment Mr. Hearst was at the absolute peak of his life.

e zest for life and vitality of
 man in his prime are evident
this study

Hearst's mornings were generally given over to business affairs while his guests explored the wonders of the estate and relaxed in these beautiful surroundings.

3 - San Simeon's
Golden Yesterdays

Life at San Simeon was strictly casual within a few set rules. Since Hearst's own hours were scheduled, the routine revolved loosely around that schedule. He usually began his day at ten or eleven in the morning, and it would frequently be two or three o'clock the next morning when he would end it. During that time, if he felt like it, he would devote eight or more hours to the work of conducting his vast empire—twenty-nine newspapers, fifteen magazines, eight radio stations, four film companies, two million acres of land, five mines, two canning factories, a retail store, vast city real estate, plus directing the activities of thirty-one thousand employees. But what made the Chief unique was that he ran his empire without any of the frenzy that often accompanies the corporate image.

By contrast, he might let business go entirely and indulge himself in the sports he favored. For a man who could afford anything, these were surprisingly simple—tennis, croquet, horseback riding, or swimming. Golf never interested him. Because of his mercurial temperament it seemed absurd to waste time chasing a little white ball up and down a golf course.

An excellent swimmer, Mr. Hearst made frequent use of his pools. But he was never far from his work. Sometimes he would come up from submergence, spouting like a porpoise, to answer one of the telephones that surrounded the beautiful Neptune Pool—in plant boxes, behind trees, or under rocks—or find his secretary, Joe Willicombe, waiting at the edge with a news teletype. He would look it over, give an order, and return to his swimming.

Whatever activity was occupying him, he would always stop long enough to go over Willicombe's day-by-day list of business matters.

Roses and a myriad of plantings enhanced the setting of many pieces of Carrara statuary, for which Hearst had a great weakness. *Below:* La Casa Grande dominated everything, even the towering palms.

Next to La Casa Grande, the Neptune Pool is the most impressive creation at San Simeon.

A fine swimmer, the owner is getting his money's worth in the huge pool.

The Chief enjoyed croquet.

And could turn easily from recreation to work.

Making notations with a soft, black pencil in his careless hand, the Chief would make decisions affecting the lives of men he had never seen— hiring and firing, settling quarrels, and directing make-up and news treatment on papers, three thousand miles away—sometimes even using a croquet mallet for a desk.

Nothing pleased Mr. Hearst more than when everybody got out-of-doors in the afternoon to take part in some group activity. The tennis tournaments were legendary, taking in everyone from various dubs to the above-average amateurs like Errol Flynn, Charlie Chaplin, and Cary Grant to such experts as Bill Tilden, Alice Marble, Fred Perry, and Helen Wills, with whom Mr. Hearst often played. Despite his size he was a remarkably good player. Dick Powell once recalled an amusing experience he had playing a set with him. When the host invited Powell to play, naturally Dick's first instinct was "to take it easy" with the older man. While Mr. Hearst did not chase balls all over the court during the game, his placement was so good that the surprised Powell was beaten in short order.

After lunch Marion Davies (left) and Bill Haines (second from right) joined the other guests to watch the tennis matches.

Bill Tilden

Charles Farrell

Robert Taylor

Proud of his horsemanship, Hearst was frequently in the saddle accompanied by Francisco "Pancho" Estrada. Pancho, born on the ranch, was a direct descendant of the family who obtained the original land grant for the San Simeon ranch in 1842. He worked all of his life for Hearst and was one of the few who could address him as "Willie."

Probably, Mr. Hearst was most famous for his picnics. Expeditions on horseback were often organized. W.R., wearing a big stiff-brimmed Castilian sombrero and astride a well-brushed palomino, with his ever-present guide, Pancho, by his side, would lead his guests on these camping trips—sometimes riding for three or four days without ever leaving the property. The servants and a portable kitchen preceded the guests and created elaborate barbecues in the wilderness.

At the end of these rides, when everyone returned to the Castle, the one least exhausted and saddle-weary was always the host himself, and he seemed to take a secret delight in the feeling that, while being senior in years, he was still the most durable. Hearst forgot to remember that he had ridden these ranges since boyhood, while most of the guests could boast of only an occasional trot on the bridle path of L.A.'s Griffith Park.

Back from a ride, the host obviously enjoyed himself and was probably the least saddle-weary.

Married at San Simeon,
Pat and Arthur Lake.

Dress at San Simeon was at all times casual. The only two exceptions were once during the visit of President and Mrs. Coolidge, and the other time for the wedding of Marion Davies' niece, Pat, to Arthur Lake of "Dagwood" fame. Always, relaxation and fun were the keynotes—there was no stuffiness or snobbishness. Mr. Hearst set great store by companions who would keep him amused. There were certain members of the crowd—particularly the funsters such as Hearst columnist Harry Crocker, William Haines, the M-G-M movie star, and the multitalented Charlie Chaplin who could break through his reserve.

While it's certain that Mr. Hearst hosted more than his share of big parties during his lifetime, it was the small gatherings with his intimate friends that he seemed to enjoy most. One of the members of that select group, former movie star William Haines, now a very successful interior decorator, attributes his whole second career to Mr. Hearst and his many, many visits to San Simeon. Haines, a great admirer of the Chief, recalls fondly:

"Once you broke the shell and you got inside the man, he was a gentle, soft, and remarkably natural person. He was a man of enormous generosity, yet he hated to be thanked for anything he gave; but he loved to get small gifts, like candy, and he would open the packages with all the delight of a child, and for all his shyness he would occasionally have flashes of homely humor. If in the mood, Mr. Hearst would even get up and entertain *us*. He loved to yodel. You know, I always felt he was a frustrated actor. I don't think it's generally known, but when he was attending Harvard, to supplement the ordinary diversions of student life, he worked in the 'Hasty Pudding' shows. He did everything—sang, played the banjo, did imitations, and even learned to dance the buck and wing. In fact, he became so stage-struck he even toyed with the prospects of an acting career. But this youthful ambition was quickly discouraged by his Victorian mother, Phoebe. She felt that acting as a profession was vulgar, if not a shade immoral. Funny, at the little parties, he used to love to do his favorite Charleston dance. As you know, he was a towering six footer—a mountainous man—and he did the Charleston like a performing elephant. He had as little grace as an elephant, but he had the *dignity* of one," Haines concluded with a smile.

Regardless of what people thought of him he was nothing of the poseur and was activated only by what interested him. Charlie Chaplin, in his autobiography, gave another insight to Hearst's character.

"Mr. Hearst, at times, was surprisingly childish and his feelings would easily be hurt. I remember one evening when we were choosing sides for a game of charades, he complained that he'd been left out. 'Well,' said Jack Gilbert facetiously, 'we'll play a charade on our own and act out the word "pillbox." I'll be the box and you can be the pill.' But W.R. took it the wrong way. His voice quivered, 'I don't want to play your old charades,' he said. And with that he left the room."

In the carefree years before World War II, the Hollywood contingent loved to ham it up as Bill Haines is doing here.

Columnist Harry Crocker engages in a bit of foolery.

No one could outmug Charlie Chaplin, here hoisted aloft by Haines along with socialite Winnie Law.

The host and movie star Marion Davies joined the fun with this deadpan pose at the '49er party.

His mother's influence was at all times evident. Even when angry or disturbed, Mr. Hearst had an innate courtesy about him. He never flew off in a yelling rage. If he ever became bored at San Simeon or uncomfortable, he would simply disappear.

Part of the daily routine for Mr. Hearst and his guests was visiting the zoo to witness the feeding of the animals. W.R.'s love of animals was one of the few constants in his life, and it was consistent with his mania for collecting that he amassed at San Simeon the largest private assemblage of the Kingdom Animalia in the world.

The mere job of logistics in providing food for the various types was staggering. For a few months in the year the grazing animals were able to maintain themselves, but the remaining time they were fed once a day. This was done by a large crew whose job it also was to have horsemeat for the lions and tigers, fish for the polar bears wallowing in their big pool, and even lettuce, carrots, apples, and nuts for the monkeys, birds, and other animals of the herbivorous species. The average black bear at San Simeon consumed daily two quarts of fresh milk, six quarts of cooked cereal, six large carrots, two heads of lettuce, and several times a week, a little meat. The only animal roaming the Enchanted Hill that did not present a nutritional problem was the camel, who is not particular about its food and is never bothered by indigestion. Its strong yellow teeth can chew nearly anything—bitter thorny shrubs, fish, bones, blankets, and even leather if it's hungry enough.

At its peak, sixty species of grazing animals and thirty species of jungle animals roamed the two thousand, fenced-in acres of San Simeon. The first field animals Hearst acquired were a herd of pure white fallow deer imported from Asia. He next added black buffaloes from Montana, musk oxen from Greenland, and emus from Australia. There were great-horned elk, prong-horned antelopes, and jumping kangaroos; hundreds of zebras, llamas, and ostriches.

Great effort was made to exclude all predatory animals such as mountain lions and wild cats who made their way into the preserve by leaping over the woven wire fences from the limbs of trees. These were the only animals ever hunted at San Simeon.

About a quarter of a mile behind La Casa Grande was the zoo where the caged animals dwelled. Joseph Schenck, the movie producer, started Mr. Hearst's collection of jungle animals with a pair of baby lions. To

A great variety of hoofed animals appeared at feeding time along the road leading to the Castle.

Wire fences had to be placed around young trees until they had grown beyond the reach of browsing livestock.

Andean llamas adapted perfectly to the climate and their heavy coats provided protection against the frequent coastal fogs.

Bears have one of the most ravenous appetites in the animal kingdom and this one was no exception.

The bison are gone but the colorful zebra may still be seen at San Simeon today.

At least three continents are represented here. The emu from Australia, a camel from Asia and in the background, sheep from North America.

These dozing yet alert foxes found the California sun to their liking.

them were added cheetahs, black panthers, spotted leopards, elephants, cockatoos, eagles, South American spider monkeys, chimpanzees, a West African porcupine, sacred monkeys from Japan, Java, and India, and even a giant turtle.

Mrs. Fremont Older, in her biography of Hearst, gives us an example of his great love and concern for animals in her story of Diana, the seal, who one day "waddled up to the warehouses and decided to adopt the ranch as her home," pleasing W.R. so much that he "abandoned national and international interests, and set his mind to work on Diana's future. By telephone he ordered a shelter to be made for her on the beach so that daily she might be fed fresh fish, and at the same time have a daily plunge in the Pacific. Soon Diana became so tame that she tried to live in the house of her keeper."

But of all the members of the animal kingdom there is strong evidence that dogs were by far his favorite. This was apparent by his lifelong fight against cruelty to animals and uncontrolled vivisection waged in his newspapers.

The human side of this complex man was never more in evidence than when he mourned publicly over the death of his dog in his column, "In the News." Answering a letter of sympathy from his old friend Dr. Frank Barham, publisher of the Los Angeles *Herald*, Hearst wrote in part:

"You know, Frank, a boy and his dog are no more inseparable companions than an old fellow and his dog. To his dog he is just as good as he ever was—maybe better, because he's more appreciative of the dog's devotion. Anyhow, the dog and the old guy understand each other and and get along 'just swell.' So I do miss Helen. I was very fond of her.

"She always slept in a big chair in my room, and her solicitous gaze followed me to bed at night, and was the first thing to greet me when I woke in the morning. Then when I arose she begged me for the special distinction of being put in my bed, and there she lay in luxurious enjoyment of the proud privilege until I was ready to leave. . . . Who could fail to be won by so much care and conscientious concern—so much attention and affection?

"Aldous Huxley says, 'Every dog thinks his master Napoleon, hence the popularity of dogs.' That is not the strict truth. Every dog adores his master notwithstanding the master's imperfections, of which it is prob-

A special bond existed between Hearst and his dachshund Helen, the closest of companions for more than fifteen years.

ably acutely aware. And its master, unless he is lower in the animal scale than the dog, responds to such devotion. . . . So as your dog loves you, you come to love your dog. . . . Love creates love, devotion inspires devotion, unselfishness begets unselfishness, and that fact is more than a commendable quality in the animal kingdom. It is an eventual hope of humanity.

"Helen died in my bed and in my arms. I have buried her on the hillside overlooking the green lawn where she used to run. . . ."

Since there were few restrictions placed on the visitors' time schedule, the one requesting the guests to gather in the great Assembly Hall at seven-thirty was adhered to rigidly. At that hour, Mr. Hearst would leave the lofty solitude of his medieval Gothic study, and enter his elegantly carved wood elevator, which had once been a confessional in an old Catholic church in Europe. Descending slowly to the ground floor precisely at the appointed hour, Hearst would move among the casually dressed guests—celebrities, Hearst executives, and eager young starlets—singling out here and there a few to chat with, while the others watched to see who was in Hearstian favor at the moment. Critics attempted to assay Hearst as a royal phenomenon, but his manner belied this. Mr. Hearst showed no kingly arrogance. His was a *presence*—an attitude of command—a man one could not ignore—and his manner was shy rather than regal. But all who witnessed that nightly entrance into the Assembly Hall were in full agreement that he was a fascinating mystery.

Irving Cobb, the noted writer, an admirer of Mr. Hearst for his genuine hospitality and pungent, witty conversation, after witnessing one of these nightly rituals, wrote an interesting comment about Hearst in *Cosmopolitan* magazine.

"I never felt I'd met the real Hearst. Mainly I beheld only his outer shell, the protective film behind which lurked a secret, aloof being, whose personal convictions were not to be fathomed, whose private viewpoints were only to be guessed at."

Cocktails were served before dinner in this enormous Assembly Hall, but Mr. Hearst did not approve of immoderate consumption of hard liquor. There was a stringent rule that there was to be no liquor in your room, and if a bottle of whisky were found, you got your marching orders down the hill. As one of his biographers pointed out: "Hearst

The Gothic Library was connected to the Assembly Hall below by an elevator, which Mr. Hearst would use to greet his guests at precisely 7:30 P.M.

While the furnishings and art treasures were virtually limitless and overpowering in the museumlike Assembly Hall, the liquor was not . . . one cocktail was the rule.

Judging from the dozens of Hollywood biographies that mention dining at San Simeon, the sheer magnificence of the Refectory never failed to overwhelm the not easily impressed movie colony set.

knew that pepole could be trusted more or less to drink in packs, but the trouble came when they foregathered in pairs or small groups behind their doors. Hence the rule: No drinking in your room."

However, it's not surprising that a large amount of conversation was given to the fascinating sport of gossiping about the Hearst estate. The behavior of the guests on the Enchanted Hill was contested at almost every dinner party in Hollywood, both in the thin air of the Hearstian devotees and the hot air of the uninitiated.

But contrary to the widespread misunderstanding about the "wild goings-on" at San Simeon, from the most reliable sources I have yet to hear of any indications of bacchanalian revelry.

Dinner was announced at nine, but Mr. Hearst would delay it if there were some interesting entertainment in progress, much to the consternation of the chef and his staff.

When you entered the great dining room, the Refectory, the pride of Mr. Hearst's collection, you had the feeling you were in a cathedral. The ceiling came from an Italian sixteenth-century monastery of the Renaissance, and has more-than-life-size figures, each representing a saint with his or her symbol. On each side of the long monastic dining tables were folding Dante chairs that could seat over sixty people. A huge fireplace stood at one end of the room, so high that three or four persons could walk into it without bending; but ultimately it had to be glassed in because of the intensity of the enormous fire, and guests who would sit "below the salt" at the end of the table would be roasted on one side.

After an incredibly plush dinner, with butlers serving from rolling trays containing almost every imaginable kind of meat and game, vegetable and salad, and enhanced with several kinds of vintage wines, Mr. Hearst would usher his guests to the Castle's fifty-seat private theatre. New prerelease features from Hollywood would be flown up, unseen by anyone outside of a few top executives. Not so well known, as this is pretty exclusive and will probably shake up the film historians, is the fact that the first audience to view the unreleased legendary *Gone with the Wind* was seated in Mr. Hearst's private theatre at San Simeon six months before its gala première in Atlanta, Georgia, on December 14, 1939.

During the screening Mr. Hearst would sit in a big leather chair on

the aisle, with a telephone alongside, with which he could not only contact the projectionist to adjust the sound, but which was also connected to the switchboard at San Simeon (known to the telephone company as "Hacienda"). It had a system of telephone trunk lines connected to all his far-flung publication centers, allowing him to talk to any of his employees within a matter of seconds.

Mr. Hearst, despite the myriad of movies he viewed at San Simeon, had very few special favorites on the screen. One of the last was Shirley Temple.

Opposite: The vast publishing network of newspapers and magazines gave Hearst unmatched power in Hollywood and never was it more vividly demonstrated than when he was furnished the first print allowed outside the studio of the legendary *Gone with the Wind*. It was seen at San Simeon months before its première in Atlanta.

W.R. was a lifelong devotee of the motion picture and one of his favorite actresses of all time was this little lady.

This was consistent with Hearst's lifelong moralistic attitude toward motion pictures. He was forever bugging Hollywood for its sexy movies. As early as October 1927, he stated editorially:

"Suggestive films and ultra-sex films have become altogether too numerous of late. Their effect on the community is bad and their re-actions on the industry is bad. The explanation of this flood of sex films is simple: that is the cheapest and easiest way of attracting the attention of a certain prurient element of the public." Considering that was in *1927*, it's interesting to contemplate what would have happened if the Chief would have lived to the age of realism in motion pictures!

That's Marie Dressler emoting under a huge load of coyote pelts with her host as Marion Davies kibitzes in this rare scene taken from a San Simeon amateur movie.

4 - Hearst and Hollywood

While I'm sure Mr. Hearst will be remembered primarily for his journalistic activities and art collecting, his involvement with motion pictures was every bit as dedicated. He was truly fascinated with the cinema all of his life.

He had been an avid photographer from the time he acquired his first box camera, and when the pictures began to move on the screen he quickly became absorbed in this embryonic medium, as he was with everything new and exciting.

I'm sure the reader can well imagine how surprised I was to learn that Mr. Hearst also liked to take home movies, and, more importantly, enjoyed appearing in them. In town he was very reticent about having his picture taken, but at San Simeon he seemed to have no objection—he'd even kid about it.

Members of the family recall that in the early days of San Simeon he even made his own amateur featurettes, actually writing and directing little stories and successfully persuading some of his famous guests to perform in these little epics.

Thanks to Mr. Hearst's son David, the author can attest to this being a fact, as I've actually seen one of Mr. Hearst's star-studded home movies. The story escapes me, but as I remember, it was a short melodrama and it had a very impressive cast. Charlie Chaplin and Louella Parsons, the noted columnist, were the hero and heroine, and they were supported by such weekend extras as Clark Gable, Carole Lombard, Gary Cooper, Mayor Walker, and Marie Dressler, among others.

But it was Hearst's inimitable talent for reaching the mass mind and his insatiable thirst to expand his newspaper audience that inevitably led him, as early as 1913, to seriously explore the possibilities of motion picture production.

He really became a pioneer when he authorized the filming of Woodrow Wilson's first inauguration on March 4, 1913, thereby making him the founder of America's first newsreel—Hearst-Selig Weekly.

He also achieved cinematic immortality when he made the first movie serial—*The Perils of Pauline*, starring the incomparable Pearl White. One of the fondest memories of my childhood was being among the whistling, stamping audiences that jammed our local nickelodeon to watch the beautiful Pearl's breath-taking adventures and daring escapes from death. Unless one lived through the era, it's impossible to appreciate the impact of Pearl White on that generation.

With the enormous success of this cliff hanger, combined with the simultaneous serialization of the same fast-moving melodrama in all his newspapers, it was only a step to full-length silent features. With Adolph Zukor, he formed the Cosmopolitan Production Company and built his first motion picture studio in 1919 in New York City. His initial effort was Fannie Hurst's *Humoresque*, starring Ramon Novarro and Alma Rubens, followed by *When Knighthood Was in Flower*, *Little Old New York*, and in 1924, *Janice Meredith*. The star of the latter three was a beautiful Ziegfeld girl named Marion Davies. It's interesting also to note that Mr. Hearst was the first to recognize the potential talent of a Broadway comedian named W. C. Fields, who played his first motion picture role in the above-mentioned silent picture, *Janice Meredith*.

In the late twenties, Hearst moved his production company to California and joined forces with M-G-M, where he made his most memorable pictures. In addition to producing *Broadway Melody*, the first musical in sound, he was responsible for *White Shadows in the South Seas*, *The Big House*, *The Floradora Girl*, *Peg o' My Heart*, *Operator Thirteen*, *Polly of the Circus*, and in 1933, *Going Hollywood*, with the current singing sensation Bing Crosby.

In the middle thirties he moved his production company to Warner Brothers, where he made a number of pictures, including *Page Miss Glory*, in which he introduced another rising young singing star named Dick Powell.

Marion Davies was Cosmopolitan's biggest star. Starting in 1922, with

The first picture W. C. Fields made was a Hearst production of *Janice Meredith* in 1924. Marion Davies, savoring the barbecue, was a former Ziegfeld Follies girl.

Miss Davies turned the tables on famed soldier Douglas MacArthur in getting his autograph when he visited her M-G-M set of *Operator 13* in 1934. Hearst was almost successful in securing a presidential nomination for the General in 1948.

While frequently disappointing at the box office, Hearst's Cosmopolitan Productions were outstanding for the opulence of their sets and costumes. Bing Crosby, serenading Cosmopolitan's main attraction, was well on his way to stardom when *Going Hollywood* was made in 1933.

An excellent process shot from *Page Miss Glory* in 1935. The specter coming between Dick Powell and Marion is Claude Rains.

Few stars worked with more of Hollywood's leading men than Marion Davies and no actress was better liked. This is from *Cain and Mabel* with Clark Gable, which Hearst's company made in 1937.

the silent picture *When Knighthood Was in Flower*, she remained the company's stellar attraction for the next two decades.

With the advent of talking pictures it was feared by some (and probably hoped for by the jealous) that Miss Davies would not be able to master the sound medium, due to a slight impediment in her speech.

One person who disagreed with the critics and cynics was Cary Grant, a close friend of both Mr. Hearst and Marion. Grant has stated that at no time did he feel any apprehension about Marion Davies' career in the talkies. He explained: "What Marion had was a charming stammer that crept into her voice when she was animated." Evidently Cary Grant's prophecy proved correct, for during the thirties Marion Davies made movies with practically every important male star in Hollywood.

Marion was one of the best-liked members of the motion picture colony. Beloved by everyone who knew her, she endowed many charities still in existence, most notably the Marion Davies Foundation's Children's Clinic at UCLA that served twelve thousand children a year in the first fifteen years.

In the late thirties the depression took its toll, and Hearst found that even for him making pictures was too expensive a luxury to continue. For more than twenty years he had been involved in his most disastrous business venture and undoubtedly his greatest disappointment (it's reported he lost $7,000,000), and only those who understood how badly he had wanted success in the motion picture industry and how confidently he had expected it could realize the extent of his frustration. His pictures were often successful artistically, but seldom financially, due to his customary lavishness with never any thought of an adequate return.

But at least the Chief had a sense of humor about it. Once at San Simeon a financier from England asked Mr. Hearst if there was any money in motion pictures. "Well, there's a lot of mine in there," the host wryly replied.

5 - Mr. Hearst Gives a Party

With San Simeon a good two hundred miles from the movie capital, Mr. Hearst built another castle more convenient to Hollywood. A little white palace on the sands of the blue Pacific at Santa Monica, it consisted of five connected Colonial houses with a total of over one hundred rooms and fifty-five bathrooms. Thirty-two servants were needed to run the place efficiently. In the center was the great three-story U-shaped main house with "more columns across the back than the Supreme Court Building in Washington." Over three hundred feet wide, it was often referred to as San Simeon in miniature.

In his planning and construction of the beach house, Hearst proceeded in the same manner as he had at San Simeon. That is, the architectural plans were drawn to accommodate antique rooms he had imported from Europe. The spacious dining room, reception room, and drawing room —each over sixty feet long—all came from Burton Hall in County Clare. The thirty-seven fireplace mantels were from English estates, and a rathskeller on the lower level had been an inn in Surrey, dating back to 1560. Throughout the house hung masterpieces of Rembrandt, Hals, Reynolds, and Rubens. In the beautiful oak-paneled library a screen rose from the floor for the inevitable movie in the evening.

The beach house did not have the pretense of a museum or a castle, but was a sunny, light, informal place, devoted to endless fun. As it was handier to Hollywood, invitations were seldom refused, and it quickly became the epicenter of the movie colony's social activities. On weekends there were always at least fifty or sixty visitors about —swimming, playing tennis, and watching movies. Guests who liked to swim had their choice of the ocean a few feet away or a beautiful hundred-foot pool with a Venetian marble bridge spanning the center of it.

The Santa Monica beach house was designed to handle some of the largest soirees the movie colony had ever seen.

Most guests chose the latter, because even Mr. Hearst couldn't keep the sea at an even temperature.

As at San Simeon, the Chief lived here at Santa Monica, much as he did everywhere else, running his empire and keeping a watchful eye on the national scene. In fact, shortly after Mr. Hearst occupied the beach house he arranged to make his first radio speech on the NBC network. The broadcasting company agreed to pick up the event by one of the first "remotes" from his luxurious library. He took the opportunity on this national hook-up to strike back at his erstwhile friend, F.D.R., whom he originally had been instrumental in placing in the White House. In reply to a criticism of the Hearst papers on one of the President's fireside chats, W.R., in a stirring patriotic speech, concluded: "The Hearst papers are never quite sure whether they can support or oppose the President's policies, because those policies change so much on their way from expression to execution.

Network radio was added to his many other means of influencing public opinion. Subject: outspoken criticism of F.D.R.'s economic policies.

"We are quite sure that we oppose Russian Communism, German Nazi-ism and French and English imperialism. We support American liberty and democracy, American freedom of the press and freedom of speech, including freedom of the President to take a few fireside shots occasionally."

As was his custom, he soon turned from national to personal matters, which always included attention to his collecting and entertaining. Unlike San Simeon, the Santa Monica house frustrated Mr. Hearst a bit. It was "finished," and even though he would occasionally rip out a room or two just for the pleasure of redesigning it and utilizing more paneling from Europe, the scope for his construction craze was limited. His "edifice complex" thus restrained, he was happiest at San Simeon.

And so, here at this manse beside the sea, he replaced his passion for building with an orgy of party giving. Though W.R. had never mastered the art of intimate friendship, he certainly possessed a host of admirers.

He began to weave his own tapestry of entertaining and knew the importance of creating a pleasing backdrop for his guests and the enchantment of make-believe.

His parties were masterpieces and they were all original, all wonderful fun. There were big parties, little parties, fantastic parties, and spectacular parties. Some simple, some gargantuan, but always gay, amusing, enjoyable. Hearst became the reigning king of entertaining in Hollywood and did it with pure pleasure. He had the know-how of a unique, highly specialized expert who created atmospheres of gaiety, elegance, and novelty that inevitably became memorable social occasions.

Elsa Maxwell, who was an expert in the field, once said: "Men are in fact better hosts than women . . . not all men, heaven knows. But if a man is a good host at all he is usually a winner. . . . William Randolph Hearst gets a Blue Ribbon."

Mr. Hearst knew that the acid test of all entertaining is the extent to which guests enjoy themselves and so he sought only to please his guests. And in doing so, he pleased himself. He also knew that one of the sure ways to achieve a successful affair was to do away with any formality, and the quickest way to disarm guests was to have them in costume. He devised some of the most ingenious events the town had ever seen.

There was the kid party, where the handsome Clark Gable came dressed as a Boy Scout and Norma Shearer and Joan Crawford were frilly little Shirley Temples. Another was the sumptuous Early American party with Mr. Hearst appearing as James Madison, another firm believer in the Constitution and gracious living, and his five sons all outfitted as sailors of our young Republic. In keeping with the theme, Norma Shearer came as Marie Antoinette, representing our French ally during the Revolution. But the *pièce de résistance* was the five-tiered cake fashioned like a replica of Independence Hall.

Another fondly remembered affair was the "Your Favorite Character from History" party, which boasted the incomparable sparkle of Doug Fairbanks, Sr., as Don Juan, with the lovely Mary Pickford, Charlie Chaplin as Napoleon, and Theda Bara as the Spanish Queen Isabella. And equally successful was his "Come as Your Favorite Movie Star" shindig, which brought Gloria Swanson as Helen Hayes in *The White Sister*, Gary Cooper as Fu Manchu, Groucho Marx as Rex the Wonder Horse, and his brother Harpo as an unlikely Rasputin.

One of the first affairs at Santa Monica was a kid's party, and Clark Gable still looked plenty masculine alongside Marion Davies.

Of course no one could touch the cake until W.R. made the first cut. Apparently his sons Randolph, George, and W.R., Jr., approve.

W.R., Jr., admiring an absolutely glowing Norma Shearer as Marie Antoinette.

Doug Fairbanks, Sr.; Mary Pickford; the host; Charlie Chaplin; and Theda Bara.

As one can well imagine, Mr. Hearst was an open-handed host and spared no expense when he entertained. The food, wines, flowers, and service were all of the finest. Naturally, such generosity was pleasing and flattering to his guests. They were treated regally, they felt like royalty for an evening, and they basked in it. In return, their host felt the glow of their vivid charm and the great warmth of their personalities and good humor, and derived great pleasure from it all.

In Mr. Hearst's long page of entertaining there is one party that stands out in memory and was perhaps the most legendary of all. It was his last and most spectacular public appearance at the beach house by the sea in 1938 when he celebrated his seventy-fifth birthday with a huge circus party attended by over three hundred people. It was a three-ring extravaganza that didn't end until the wee hours of the morning. The double tennis courts were tented over with a gigantic circus big top, there was a full scale merry-go-round that was in continuous motion, and a raucous hurdy-gurdy added to the excitement. But, of course, the thing that makes parties is people, and the greater variety of people, the better the affair, and this one outdid all others.

The host had the time of his life as the ringmaster. Cowboys and cowgirls were in abundance—Clark Gable, Carole Lombard, Dick Foran, Rochelle Hudson, Sonja Henie, Patsy Kelly, Joel McCrea and his wife, Frances Dee, movie mogul Jack Warner and his wife, Ann, Arthur Lake and his pretty Pat, and Tom Brown with Natalie Draper, whose father, Ted Draper, was a Hearst executive with the Los Angeles *Herald-Express*.

There were Indians too, most notable, former All-American football star, Johnny Mack Brown, and his pretty wife, Connie, who came as the Big Chief and his squaw.

Bette Davis came as a bearded lady, Mary Carlisle and Anita Louise as petite bareback riders. Of course there was a fabulous array of clowns—Henry Fonda, sad-faced in white tights; Norman Foster, the director, as the immortal tramp Joe Jackson; Pat O'Brien as a large-nosed Harlequin; and such merry buffoons as James Stewart, Van Johnson, and George Jessel. Impresario Sid Grauman was a pitchman with the side show, and Bill Haines, a high-wire performer, later did a magic act with Marion Davies in which her head wound up in a basket. Frances Marion, the brilliant screenwriter, came as an oriental charmer and Hedda

Kicking off the most fabulous party of them all, the host and ring-master officiates at the pastry.

Hopper as a fearless animal trainer. Dr. and Mrs. Griffin, the lovely Irene Dunne, attended, he as a Keystone Kop and she as the mistress of a trained animal act. And you couldn't miss Dolores del Rio as a stunning bareback rider on the arm of her husband, Cedric Gibbons, the noted M-G-M art designer.

Big stars of the silent screen also graced the affair—beauteous Claire Windsor, Ramon Novarro, Aileen Pringle, Dorothy MacKaill, Jack Mulhall, Constance Talmadge, Louise Fazenda with her producer husband, Hal Wallis, and Eileen Percy with her mate, songwriter Harry Ruby.

There was one table filled with Hearst executives—Louella Parsons with her husband, Dr. Harry Martin, and the man she sent her columns

The massed balloons were but one example of the incredible planning of these affairs.

to, George C. Young, publisher of the Los Angeles *Examiner*, Bill Curley, editor of the New York *Journal-American*, Walter Howey, editor of the Chicago *Herald-Examiner*, and Mr. Hearst's supersecretary, Joe Willicombe.

Joe Willicombe was the one man closest to W. R. Hearst and one of the least publicized. He was a former New York *American* reporter who found himself in one of the country's toughest jobs because he knew shorthand. For twenty-two years as the Chief's perennial Man Friday, Willicombe was required to mold his life to his employer's, be on call day and night, be ready to travel at a moment's notice, submerge his own individuality, and keep himself strictly in the shadow of the

Everybody's favorite clown, Ed Wynn.

The irrepressible Bill Haines gets a laugh with the help of Marion Davies.

Mr. and Mrs. Johnny Mack Brown in from the reservation.

Mary Carlisle and David Hearst make a strikingly attractive couple.

In the center ring, a pensive Dolores del Rio.

Although she never worked for him as a columnist, Hedda Hopper was one of Hearst's dearest friends.

Bob Montgomery and Jean Muir getting the lowdown from Walter Winchell.

Allan Jones and his pretty wife (Irene Hervey) go merrily around.

Irene Dunne, George Jessel, Sally Blane, and Norman Foster.

powerful man, and his influence became enormous. He was the single link between Hearst executives and their Chief and was the final judge as to whom Mr. Hearst would or would not see.

Another great favorite was Walter Howey, who previously had been the editor of the Chicago *Tribune*, making a salary of eight thousand dollars a year. Rumor has it he was lured away by a Hearst offer of thirty-five thousand to become the legendary city editor of the Chicago *Herald-Examiner*. Howey gained immortality of a sort when he became the prototype for the irrepressible managing editor in the Broadway play *The Front Page*, written by Ben Hecht and Charles Mac-Arthur.

On this festive night, the hit of the evening was Mervyn LeRoy as master of an exciting acrobatic troup called the Flying San Simeons, which included such daredevils as Cary Grant and Randolph Scott.

Others sitting around the huge circus ring watching the guests dance to the music of Tommy Dorsey and his band were Walter Winchell, actress Jean Muir, Bebe Daniels and Ben Lyon, Mr. and Mrs. Jules

The music was by the old pro Tommy Dorsey and his boys.

Brulatour (Hope Hampton), gorgeous Loretta Young, David Niven, Mary Astor, Jean Parker, pretty Mary Brian with Richard Watts, drama critic of the New York *Journal-American,* Stu Erwin and his wife, beautiful June Collyer, Mr. and Mrs. Leslie Howard and their son, Ronald, Joan Bennett, the personable Jimmy Shields, William Powell, Paulette Goddard, and famous reporter Adela Rogers St. Johns.

Enjoying the ride on the mammoth merry-go-round were Dolores del Rio, Marion Davies, and Mr. and Mrs. Allan Jones (Irene Hervey), parents of the great singing star Jack Jones.

Incidentally, if some of the present-day young stars could have been at this party they would have seen their parents having a marvelous time "cutting a rug." Mr. and Mrs. Robert Montgomery, parents of the "Bewitched" television star, Elizabeth Montgomery, were there. Mr. and Mrs. Henry Fonda, parents of the tremendously talented Peter and Jane, enjoyed themselves, and Mr. and Mrs. John Farrow (Maureen O'Sullivan), parents of the provocative Mia, were taking a chance on the wheel of fortune.

Claudette Colbert, alias Pocahontas.

The Pat O'Briens sitting one out.
George C. Young, publisher of the Los Angeles *Examiner*, and his
star columnist, Louella Parsons; her husband, Dr. Harry Martin; together with Irene Dunne and her husband, Dr. Griffin. (That's Clark
Gable and Carole Lombard exiting right.)

At ringside, Stu Erwin and wife (June Collyer), Richard Watts, New York drama critic, and sparkling Mary Brian.

Marion Davies taking a turn.

Admirers of bearded lady Bette Davis are Ian Hunter and Andy Lawler.

In the center ring, the Flying San Simeons. From left, Cary Grant, Mervyn LeRoy, unidentified man, Mrs. Hal Roach, Hal Roach, Sally Eilers (Mrs. Harry Joe Brown), Mrs. Milton Bren, Randolph Scott, Florence Lake, Harry Joe Brown, Townsend Netcher, Milton Bren, and Marion Davies in the foreground.

Joe Willicombe, Hearst's right-hand man, in the pretty clutches of Dorothy MacKaill.

The legendary editor Walter Howey with director Raoul Walsh.

The British were represented by the Leslie Howards and son, Ronald.

Dolores del Rio, one of Hollywood's great beauties.

Mary Astor, David Niven, Loretta Young, and "young friend."
Back row: Douglass Montgomery, Leslie Howard, Marion Davies,
unidentified. Front row: Bruce Cabot, George K. Arthur, Ramon
Novarro, and Eileen Percy.

Mr. and Mrs. John Farrow (Maureen O'Sullivan) looking for a lucky number.

Chester Morris and the Bob Montgomerys.

Look closely and you will recognize Henry Fonda behind that make-up. With him is Mrs. Fonda (Frances Brokaw). Parents of Jane and Peter.

And all of Mr. Hearst's five sons were there, George as a clown, and Bill, Jr., Jack, David, and Randolph as weight lifters. W.R. was a good father and he deeply loved his children. With them he was completely relaxed and was his most natural self, and they idolized him. The boys are their father's sons. I can pay them no greater compliment.

After all the guests had enjoyed a piece of the fantastic birthday cake—three tiers in the shape of a giant circus tent with all the traditional characters and animals parading around it—and before the "circus" left town, everyone stood and toasted their host on his seventy-fifth birthday. The date was April 29, 1938.

By contrast, the festivities for Mr. Hearst's eightieth birthday were simple, celebrated on his beloved Enchanted Hill, attended only by his sons, their wives, and a very few Hollywood friends. As he stood up in his favorite room, the Refectory, in response to the toasts from members of the party clustered in the center of the long table, with rows of unoccupied chairs on each side, it was apparent he was not overjoyed at touching the fourscore mark, and he made a graceful little speech telling why.

No affair was complete without the shot of the Chief and his boys. From left: George; W.R., Jr.; Jack; David; and Randolph.

"I shall not pretend that I'm happy to be eighty. I would gladly exchange that marker for two lifetimes at forty. Just as a woman reaching forty would gladly exchange that milestone for two at the twenty mark. Yet I am thankful and grateful that I find so much in life that is fresh, stimulating, and dear to me."

William Randolph Hearst died April 14, 1951. He was born before the Battle of Gettysburg and saw the first railroad built across the nation. He watched the motorcar replace the horse and buggy. He attended the birth of aviation and recognized its news value in August 1929 when he agreed to sponsor and finance the first globe-encircling flight of the Graf Zeppelin—if it would take off and land in the United States. It did and actually flew over San Simeon. He rounded out a full, unique, and influential life and lived to see the Atomic Age. He was eighty-eight years old.

To the end of his life he remained an enigma. Despite his lifelong philosophy, "Pleasure is worth what you can afford to pay for it," William Randolph Hearst left an estate of over $400,000,000.

Belying his years, Hearst ended the evening looking tremendously fit and full of its pleasures.

6 - San Simeon Revisited

In the golden days of San Simeon the public could only get glimpses of the Castle from a coin-in-the-slot telescope at the village below, some five miles away. This generation is more fortunate. When in the spring of 1958 the great Hearst Castle was opened to the public it gave everyone the opportunity of viewing at firsthand a combination palace and museum such as the world has rarely seen.

Today, as an immensely popular California State Historical Monument, San Simeon is open house for everyone in the world . . . including me.

Something very personal brought me back to the Enchanted Hill after many years. I'd spent a lifetime as a member of the show-business fraternity and almost the same amount of time as a member of America's largest hobby group, amateur photography. And today a film of mine, a brief chronicle of the glory days of Mr. Hearst's residence here, was to start being shown to all the tourists in the Castle's private theatre.

Now, before anyone gives me credit for having foresight in taking and collecting these pictures all through the years, I have to admit it was an accident. When I came West as a vaudeville actor in 1927, it was my first time away from home. I was very close to my mom and pop, but I hated to write letters—still do—so instead of sending back post cards and snapshots, I bought one of those newfangled 16mm home movie cameras. I left the projector at home and from time to time I would send back films of the trip. Naturally, when I got to Hollywood I wanted to take as many pictures of movie stars as I could so I'd be a big man back in Utica, New York. Yes, whenever I see a tourist with a camera, I have an inkling what motivates him.

The first big movie star I photographed was my boyhood idol, Douglas Fairbanks, Sr. Fairbanks came backstage opening night with some friends, including Charlie Chaplin, to compliment Edmund Breese, the headliner at the Orpheum Theatre, where I was also playing on the bill.

I was also lucky the next day to get some film of Charlie Chaplin doing some of his routines at the United Artists studio.

So began my personal history of Hollywood—in a tin can.

It was not until later when I started to work in pictures that I met my good friend Arthur Lake, who in a great many ways is responsible for this book. He was the one who introduced me to Mr. Hearst and made possible much of the film that is now showing at San Simeon.

I really got a camera hold on Hollywood during the long seven-year-run of my stage show, *Ken Murray's Blackouts*. It offered me the opportunity to meet virtually every star in town. Naturally, I got some great footage during that time, catching Hollywood in the act of being itself.

It was in the course of this hobby in chronicling the lives, pleasures, and activities of the Hollywood stars that my special film on San Simeon came about. And now, from what was intended to be a sort of a personal film diary of friends and neighbors I had known in Hollywood through the years, today I find myself tagged with such grandiose titles as "Hollywood Historian" and "Keeper of the Archives," etc. Of course, through the years, in other quarters I'm sure there were those who marked me as "some kind of a nut" with a bad case of delayed adolescence for having collected several thousand miles of film by roaming the movie capital, inside the studios and stars' homes, turning my camera on everything that interested me. For the opinions of this group, whose merits will not be weighed here, my answer is, it's not easy to capture in words the impressions by which your youth was molded.

I have lived and been a part of an era that has produced a whole industry of heroes and heroines—movie stars that in those days were better known to young America than most fictional folk heroes. They were the royalty of America, some of the most glamorous personalities on the world stage, and their daily comings and goings fed the imagination of the entire globe. And now, as Hollywood becomes historical, fighting to preserve the glamorous traditions that made it great, a pause is not out of order for reminiscence and remembrance for the period when ninety million people went to the "picture show" every week, and American movies probably exerted more power over more minds than any agency before or since.

Unfortunately, there has been very little worthwhile and accurate documentation of this period. For some reason Hollywood is afflicted with total amnesia when it comes to recalling anything that happened more than twenty-four hours ago. As Ezra Goodman, the film historian, puts it, "If you're thinking further back than today in the motion picture industry you're living in the past and you'll occasion a good many amusedly raised eyebrows, somewhat as if you had lost your intellectual trousers."

But the fact remains that I like the era and I like the people, and in my pictures I do try to recapture the excitement of the past, though that doesn't mean I live in it. Rather than just an exercise in nostalgia, I would like to feel there's a purpose to my film.

An individual as he stands at any moment is the product of his past, the past he has inherited and the past which he has lived. In other words, he is a bundle of memories accumulated through the experience of the race through life and through his own experiences as a person. Everyone supplies from his own experience; my pictures merely open the door.

It occurred to me along this line that the special film I had on San Simeon might be of interest and open an exciting door for the visitors who now come to the monument to see the Castle for the first time.

I mentioned this to Governor Reagan, who happens to be a very old and good friend of mine. He immediately sparked to the idea, as did William Penn Mott, Jr., the director of Parks and Recreation, Bob Meyer, Mott's deputy, and Dick Thompson, the public information officer. Very quickly after that, all the arrangements were made, and because of this I have now come back to San Simeon after these many years to attend the first showing to tourists of the film I had made.

We were met by a very friendly man, Wes Cater, who is in charge of the monument, and his supervisor of guides, Mrs. Irene Hanks. I assured them that neither I nor my party wanted any kind of special treatment. What we really preferred was to go along with a party of tourists and see San Simeon with them, sharing in the interests and excitement I felt such a group was bound to have.

However, on the side, I did ask Wes Cater a favor. I asked him if, at the conclusion of the tour, while the folks were watching my film, it would be possible for me to get a look inside the one place that no one ever sees. There is one building in this magnificent panorama where no one ever visits or takes pictures and chances are never will. It was the first guesthouse built at San Simeon in 1919, called La Casa del Mar, the House of the Sea. It's the place where Mr. Hearst lived while the Castle was being built and it was also the last house he lived in here at San Simeon.

When late in life he became ill and was unable to live conveniently in the Castle itself, he retired to La Casa del Mar and stayed there until that illness took him away and to his death. After Mr. Hearst was gone and San Simeon became a State Historical Monument, La Casa del Mar remained in the family and to this day only members of the Hearst family have any access to it.

There was a long pause, and for a moment I thought maybe I had gone too far and put Wes on a spot in asking this special favor that no other visitor had ever received. But then the eyes of this very understanding man warmed and I realized that he knew how much a visit to La Casa del Mar would mean to me in completing the story. He simply said, "I'll make the arrangements," as he walked back with me to where the group of tourists was forming.

There were fifty of us, including my wife, Bette Lou, my two teen-age daughters, Pam and Janie, my sister Dorothy and my younger son Cort. We then joined my good friend Bob Cummings, who had made the trip up from Hollwood for the occasion. We were all just in time to hear the opening remarks of our charming guide, Mrs. Hanks, as the tour party paused at the steps leading up to the Neptune Pool:

Let us begin your visit to the Hearst San Simeon State Historical Monument with an expression of warm welcome. We hope you will find it a pleasant and enriching personal experience. As you will soon discover, the Castle, as people refer to it, is not arranged as a museum nor actually as a home, although it has been both.

THE NEPTUNE POOL *Our first stop on the tour is undoubtedly a sight you'll never forget. Here you see one of the most impressive settings on the Hill. The magnificent Neptune Pool. It contains 345,000 gallons of mountain spring water in a basin 104 feet long, whose depth graduates from 3 feet 6 inches to 9 feet 6 inches. It is the largest outdoor heated swimming pool in the world. It is perfectly constructed of white marble studded with antique-green marble mosaics. On the right you see the graceful colonnades that circle the ends of the pool. On the left are a group of statues representing Venus rising from the water with mermaids and cherubs surrounding her, done for Mr. Hearst in Paris by Charles Cassou. The marble is mostly from Vermont. This way, please . . .*

LA CASA DEL SOL   The guesthouse above you is one of the three museum-like guest structures on the Hill. It's called La Casa del Sol—the House of the Sun —because the living-room windows face the sunset over the sea. The theme of this house is Moorish. The tiles around the doors and the tile seen on the base of the chimney are antique Persian, but those under the eaves were designed and made here in California, as were the iron doors. It is faced with seventeenth-century Spanish and Italian ironwork, and features a loggia ceiling from Spain and a lamp from eighteenth-century France. The concrete decoration was designed and cast here on the Hill. When great classical originals were unobtainable, statues such as the bronze copy of Donatello's David, standing atop this seventeenth-century Italian fountain, were often displayed.

The above picture, taken during construction, will give you a slight idea of the extremely difficult task of building on the edge of this steeply sloping hillside a structure three stories high on its outer side and but one on the other. Finished in 1921, La Casa del Sol is the largest guesthouse. On its three levels it boasts eight bedrooms, eight bathrooms, and two living rooms. The long-forgotten photographer was apparently standing on the exact spot where the Neptune Pool is located today.

LA CASA DEL MONTE *Our next stop is the second guesthouse built on the Hill, La Casa del Monte, named for the view afforded from the windows. This building faces the Santa Lucia Mountains. It consists of four bedrooms, four baths, a vestibule, and living room, and contains furnishings mainly of Mediterranean background from the fifteenth through the eighteenth century. The windows feature elaborate cornices rather than drapes. The tile floors are covered with Persian carpets. The chests, Chinese and Persian urns, needlework, desks, tables and chairs, and fireplaces indicate antiquity, but the decorative doors, window frames, ceilings, and floors are deceptive. They were almost entirely created in mold shops and carpenter shops here on the Hill in the 1920s. The gold leaf and paints were applied to the plaster ceilings after they were installed by European as well as local artisans.*

One bedroom is particularly impressive. It contains the bed of the great
French statesman Cardinal Richelieu. It is described by historians as: "carved and
gilt walnut; Lombardic, late sixteenth century." The headboard is carved to
simulate a canopy of fringed drapery and in the center is a coat of arms of three
fishes surmounted by a coronet and a bishop's hat.

There is a charming story regarding the tiny elaborately carved chairs on each
side of a sixteenth-century Florentine lectern in the vestibule. They originated in
Italy when ladies were wearing bouffant skirts and could not sit in armchairs.

See the things you learn in this book—a chair designed for milady's
fashions some four hundred years ago.

TERRACE AND MAIN ENTRANCE, LA CASA GRANDE *As we leave La Casa del Monte, you can now see on the hill directly above this guesthouse the main castle, La Casa Grande. Surmounted by two Spanish Renaissance towers, one hundred and thirty-seven feet high, in which hang thirty-six bronze carillon bells, the structure's façade has frequently been compared to those of Europe's historic cathedrals.*

Here on the main terrace, the marble benches, lamp standards and coping around the fish pond are the work of Cardini of Lucca, Italy, and San Francisco. The Carrara marble statue in the pond, Galatea on a Dolphin, *is of unknown origin but contemporary carving.*

Before you is La Casa Grande, the museum-home and entertainment center whose structure is modern, but whose appearance deliberately suggests a Mediterranean origin—largely Spanish.

The main entrance is fashioned like a Gothic cathedral, with the sixteenth-century limestone portraits of St. Peter and St. Paul guarding the door. The Virgin and Child in the niche high above and the mounted figure, Horseman Out for the Hunt, just below are both from the Gothic period. Through those beautiful iron-grilled doors, which once stood in a sixteenth-century Spanish convent, passed, at different times, Winston Churchill, George Bernard Shaw, Charles Lindbergh, President and Mrs. Calvin Coolidge, the Shah of Iran, General Douglas MacArthur, Sir Thomas Lipton, and countless personalities of the worlds of entertainment, politics, and journalism between 1925 and 1951.

THE VESTIBULE As you enter the vestibule of La Casa Grande, the first thing to claim your attention is the historic marble mosaic floor, dating from the first century B.C. *On your left is Jean Gérôme's statue of* Pygmalion and Galatea, *and behind it hangs a Gobelin tapestry from the renowned* History of Alexander *set and comes from the collection of Mr. Hearst's mother, Phoebe Apperson Hearst.*

The thing that caught my eye was an old whitened ox skull on the floor in front of these beautiful artifacts. Upon inquiry, I learned that Mr. Hearst found it on the ranch when he was building San Simeon and placed it in the vestibule for good luck, where it has remained ever since.

THE ASSEMBLY ROOM   *As we walk through the marble doorway, sculpted by Sansovino and bearing the crests of "the Warrior Pope," Julius II, we are now in the immense living room, the breath-taking Assembly Hall, as it is called.*

Its dimensions—eighty-four feet long, thirty-two feet wide, and twenty-two feet high—were dictated by the size of its wood-carved antique ceiling brought over from the Palazzo Mantinengo in Brescia, Italy.

Though comfortably furnished with overstuffed chairs and sofas, the room literally abounds with precious art objects. The splendid mantel-over-mantel sixteenth-century French Renaissance fireplace, probably the most impressive of the forty-one on the Hill, was constructed for the Château le Jour and came from the collection of Stanford White, the well-known American architect. At San Simeon it was used as the main source of heat in this Assembly Room. The busts above it were done by F. Duquesnoy (1593–1643).

The magnificent tapestries on the long walls are four of the Scipio set, woven in Brussels in 1550. They were designed by Giulio Romano and one of these tapestries alone is worth $400,000. The tapestries on the end walls are from drawings by Peter Paul Rubens and portray The Triumph of Religion *and* Venus and Neptune.

The floor is teakwood done in parquet design and the rugs are Persian. On the large Italian table in front of the fireplace are four silver Renaissance candlesticks, and between them sits a gorgeous jewel box made in France in the sixteenth century. It is of ebony and gilt bronze, with windows of rock crystal, and, according to experts, is one of four such cases in the world today. The bronze figure on the table in the north end of the room is Nymph Drinking *by Seifert, a German sculptor.*

Ranged on the lower walls around the entire room are a group of ancient wooden choir stalls that once stood in a centuries-old Italian monastery.

This is the room where the guests would gather informally at about 7:00 every evening. Promptly at 7:30, Mr. Hearst would descend from his Gothic Suite in his private elevator, silently enter through a secret panel on the left side of the fireplace, and suddenly appear in the room to greet his guests, and enjoy a social period. When dinner was announced at 9:00, Mr. Hearst would usher his guests through this door on the right side of the fireplace into the Refectory, as we are doing now.

I just had to ride in Mr. Hearst's elevator, and Irene Hanks obliged.

THE REFECTORY *Of all the rooms in La Casa Grande, Mr. Hearst was most proud of this great dining hall, the Refectory. In this room, more than elsewhere, we might pay respect to the architect of this building, Julia Morgan. It was she, as much as the authentic Gothic choir stalls and other artifacts of church origin, who gave this room its lofty dignity. Almost everything from the floor of Italian travertine, the tall five hundred-year-old choir stalls from Catalonia, and the high Gothic arch windows, point to the ceiling from sixteenth-century Italy with its life-sized carvings of the saints.*

Flutterng by the windows on high are colorful sixteenth-century Palio banners representing various parishes in the city of Siena, Italy, and used to this day in a religious festival featuring a horse race about the city square. The winner's banners were returned to the cathedral and hung until the next Palio Day.

Covering almost the entire walls between the banners and the seventeenth-century English refectory tables below are huge sixteenth-century Flemish tapestries done in the Gothic period style. Each tapestry portrays two scenes having to do with events from the life of the Prophet Daniel and his encounters with King Nebuchadnezzar of Babylon.

In this room is a king's ransom in silver. Mr. Hearst had the finest collection of antique silver in the world, and this dining hall just glows with it. On the sideboard to the right you can see four very valuable spike-top candlesticks from a matching set of eight, seventeenth-century French. They are standing among Irish silver-covered platters, Sheffield serving trays, and an exquisite Irish mace, circa 1867, probably made in Dublin. However, the prize of this whole collection is the beautiful oval wine cistern made by David Williams, London 1710.

Of course, dominating this impressive room is the long monastic refectory table where Mr. Murray and Mr. Cummings are seated—incidentally, in allowing them to do so we have waived one of the strictest of our rules. These priceless sixteenth-century Dante chairs are of antique walnut and the leather seats and backs are covered with Italian velvet in pomegranate design known as the velvet of the Doges.

Now, if Mr. Murray and Mr. Cummings will stop admiring that beautiful eighteenth-century Sheffield platter and favor us with their company, we will proceed to the Morning Room.

THE MORNING ROOM As you can see, right off the Refectory is the Morning Room. Its function is more or less as a back parlor. It is located in the rear of the ground floor of La Casa Grande, in close proximity to the kitchen. Therefore, guests would order their breakfast here, which would ultimately be served in the impressive dining room.

In the foreground to the right you can see one of the two Spanish Renaissance braziers, dated 1615. They were originally used to heat rooms by filling the brass bowls with burning coals.

On the table is an Irish silver covered wine platter, one of a set of three—the other two are in the Refectory.

The walls in this room are cast tile, a Kermanshah carpet covers the floor of stone tile, and the fireplace is French Gothic from the fourteenth or fifteenth century.

Since this charming room faces the rising sun, it was appropriately named.

If you're wondering about the fire burning in the fireplace, this picture was taken in 1929 at the time Mr. Hearst was enjoying the comforts of his new home.

THE KITCHEN   This is the kitchen in La Casa Grande's south wing, which also contains the service quarters. Although there are no priceless art objects in the kitchen, this room is nevertheless one of the most interesting in the house. One can imagine the activity and excitement that must have gone on in this domain from the early hours of the morning until late in the evening, especially when the guest rooms were filled to capacity.

The equipment would be a delight to any culinary devotee. It includes an oil-burning range, three baking ovens, four warming ovens, steam tables, charcoal broiler and rotisseries, an electric range with three spits, three electric tier ovens, bread and roll warmer, steamer, and steam pressure pot. In the huge pantry are stainless steel tables, a draught beer dispenser, a jumbo bread box, medicine cabinets, sinks with unusually fancy gold rooster faucet handles, and innumerable cupboards for the storage of linen, silver, and glassware and dishes, all of hotel size. There is a walk-in refrigerator for meat and three vegetable coolers downstairs. The other refrigerators are converted iceboxes. Cooking was done on oil and charcoal ranges initially and eventually on these ranges and electric stoves.

As you can imagine, there was a large staff here at the Castle. There was a head chef, a first assistant chef, a pastry cook, a head butler, from four to six waiters, and a special cook for servants. These, of course, were in addition to a head housekeeper, three maids, two houseboys, an electrician, a telegrapher, and three telephone operators, working in shifts so that there was continuous twenty-four-hour service. If more than thirty guests were accommodated, additional help would be flown up from Hollywood. Mrs. O'Brien, the housekeeper, estimated that it cost over $5000 a day to run the Castle with a full complement of guests.

That chef must have had a ball preparing the menus. He could take full advantage of what was raised on the Hill—prize Holsteins and Jerseys grazing on a splendid dairy farm. And he had his pick of corn-fed beef, spring lamb, and all kinds of pork from blue ribbon winners. The poultry ranch had all the standard breeds plus such exotics as Cornish fowl, wild turkey, and several varieties of pheasant. He could also pick up the telephone and order shrimp from New Orleans, lobster from Maine, and other food from any place in the country to prepare epicurean delights for the discerning Mr. Hearst and his guests.

MENU

La Cuesta Encantada ✦ San Simeon, California

Dinner

July 4, 1946

FRIED OLYMPIC OYSTERS

ROAST PARTRIDGE   GRAVY

BREAD CRUMBS   BREAD SAUCE

ARTICHOKES HOLLANDAISE

CAKE   CHERRY ICE CREAM

****

MOVIE

"The Perfect Marriage"

Para.

David Niven   Loretta Young

Also

Paramount Short

Breakfast 9:00 to 12:00   Luncheon 2:00   Dinner 9:00

THE ROMAN POOL *As we descend to a lower level in the back of La Casa Grande, we come to one of the most remarkable features of San Simeon today, the indoor salt-water swimming pool. It wasn't used as much as one would imagine, probably because of the outdoor Neptune Pool.*

This Roman Pool is eighty-four feet long and forty feet wide—big enough to accommodate two full-size tennis courts on its roof above. In the center may be seen the alcove that is known as the Children's Pool.

The interior is designed to suggest the atmosphere of the Roman bath and the oversized statues are reproductions of classic Greek and Roman figures. Perhaps most impressive of all are the tiles that cover the walls, floor, and central diving platform. They were made in the famous Murano kilns of Venice—many of them faced with gold—and crews of artisans were brought from Italy to lay the thousands of tiles in intricate patterns. It took well over three years to build this breath-taking structure at a cost exceeding $1,000,000.

The completion of the children's section in the Roman Pool was the last major undertaking on the Hill. At first, salt was added to fresh water but later a pumping system was installed to bring the salt water directly from the ocean seven miles away. Hearst was a man who got things done.

THE DUPLEX SUITE *We are now on the second floor in one of the small guest suites known as the Duplex with this sixteenth-century Spanish bed on the upper level and the sitting room below. It is arranged, as were most of the rooms of La Casa Grande, to house the artifacts and furnishings you see. Some, like the ceiling, columns, and balustrade above are built in.*

The ceiling was painted 250 years ago by Jean Baptiste Van Loo and depicts The Departure of Phoebus. *On the left wall hangs a seventeenth-century royal Gobelin tapestry,* The Faun. *Directly below is a porcelain beaker vase resting on a sixteenth-century Italian cabinet.*

See, they even had split-level living back in those days. Notice the rope hanging to the right of the stairs—it was used in lieu of a banister. Recommended for anyone who likes a pink marble bathroom with gold fixtures.

THE DELLA ROBBIA SUITE We next come to one of the four Cloister Suites that run through the center of this second floor in the Castle.

This entire room is dominated by works of art of the members of the Della Robbia family, after whom this suite was named. These sculptured creations of terra-cotta covered with an opaque glaze were made in the late fifteenth and early sixteenth centuries. The figured reliefs are sometimes white against a blue background, but often display a variety of colors, and the great wreaths are known the world over.

Della Robbia works in this room include on the right wall a plaque (stemma) with shield and stars; on the left, over the French Louis XII fireplace, is a bas-relief of St. Joseph and Child, flanked by a pair of sixteenth-century Spanish angel candleholders.

The designs of the sixteenth-century Spanish ceiling were copied in the door and window casings and baseboards by artisans here at San Simeon. A Persian rug from Kashan covers the floor of Italian travertine. On the right wall above the seventeenth-century Spanish library table is the painting Immaculate Conception, *attributed to Murillo. The beds are walnut with arcaded headboards and vase finials on the four posts.*

Every time I see this room I'm reminded of a story that Bill Haines told me. He had an amusing experience when he stayed here. He said that behind that bathroom door on the left he found a beautiful, fascinating picture hanging. Mr. Hearst happened to come into the room soon thereafter and Haines asked him what it was, and W.R. said it was a Goya. Laughingly the Chief added, "I wonder who put that there," and tucked the painting under his arm, and later hung it on a wall in one of the guesthouses.

THE MAIN LIBRARY   There are two libraries in La Casa Grande, this one
on the second floor for the guests, adjoining the Cloister Suites and one on the
third floor in Mr. Hearst's Gothic Suite.

This library is built directly over the Assembly Room. It duplicated the
length and width of the room below (about 84 by 32), but not the height, the
library being lower. Here you again see a magnificent Hispano-Moresque ceiling.
The teakwood floor is covered by two Tabriz hunting carpets and a Meshed.

In this beautifully paneled room above the bookcases and on tables at either
end are Grecian and Etruscan urns dating from the second through the eighth
century B.C. They are part of the over four hundred Mr. Hearst once owned,
comprising at that time the largest private collection in America. Over sixty
of them are now in the Metropolitan Museum in New York, and thirty or more
are in the Los Angeles County Museum.

On these bookshelves behind the grilled doors is a magnificent collection of rare books, manuscripts, and autographs which Mr. Hearst had gathered over fifty years, and which touched high points of American history, biography, and literature. There are letters of William Penn and Benjamin Franklin, manuscripts by Longfellow, Poe, Mark Twain, and an enormous collection of Washingtoniana.

Of all the rooms in the Castle this is my favorite. There are over five thousand volumes in this beautiful library, and though these were some of Mr. Hearst's most prized possessions, he insured none of them, stating philosophically that "no money could begin to cover their loss."

THE GOTHIC STUDY This is perhaps one of the most impressive rooms on the Enchanted Hill. Here the co-ordinated talents of the architect and muralist and the creative expression of five centuries are brought together to form a most beautiful setting.

The arches were painted by Camille Solon, who was the director and designer of murals and other works of art at the Castle from 1925 to 1940, and illustrate mythological and biblical events. From the warmth of the Bakhtiari carpets to the colors of the antique Spanish ceiling, the room is opulent yet subdued.

Above the grilled Florentine-style bookcases is an array of antique statues, lecterns, and icons. The collection of tankards and ceremonial cups, seen between the upper and lower bookcases, include German, Dutch, English, Italian, Spanish, Flemish, Russian, French, and Persian works in silver, gold,

ivory, and ceramic. The tall delicate torchères have been fitted as floor lamps with shades made from Gregorian chant book pages.

At the far end of the room, below the only oil painting ever done of Mr. Hearst, is the long mahagony table where W.R. and members of his staff conducted the business of his far-flung empire.

That portrait of the Chief, when he was thirty-one, by Orrin Peck really dominates this room. The cool blue eyes still stare out at you in lifelike intensity.

THE GOTHIC SUITE   This is Mr. Hearst's bedroom in the Gothic Suite on the third floor. One of its most striking features is the ceiling painted in geometrical designs on pine, embellished with coat of arms. It is from the Spanish castle Marchino.

The French baldachin bed—fifteenth-sixteenth century—is of oak with each post carved in a different design. Beside the bed is a twelfth-century Persian vase from Sultanabad. Above this are two portraits of Senator George Hearst, father of the publisher. On the south wall is a portrait of his mother, Phoebe Apperson Hearst, one of the great ladies of California, cofounder of the PTA, benefactress of the University of California at Berkeley, and in whose name the Enchanted Hill was contributed to the state and whose memory was its inspiration.

It is interesting to note a small, insignificant painting sitting on his chest of drawers. Not just another Madonna, it is an early fourteenth-century work by Segna, a masterpiece of Renaissance painting, and probably the single most valuable item on the estate.

Unquestionably, the biggest surprise a visitor experiences as he enters this room is the relatively small amount of space that Mr. Hearst utilized for his own sleeping quarters. Of the thirty-eight bedrooms in the 48,734 square feet of the Castle, his personal bedroom occupies the least amount of floor space—a mere 18 by 20 feet. Considering all the opulence he lavished on his guests, this is an intriguing, paradoxical side of the man.

Just across the hall from this room (not seen in our picture) is Mr. Hearst's two-sectioned bathroom done in pink marble. All the fixtures are gold-plated, even the drain pipes. The tub is 6 foot 3 inches because Hearst was.

THE CELESTIAL SUITE Here on the fourth and top floor of the Castle is the Celestial Suite, which is in the form of two bed chambers, looking out to the ocean in front and the mountains behind, with a connecting sitting room.

This sitting room between the north and south bedrooms has a ceiling, though impressive, of local origin. It is made of wood with plaster trim, painted and gilded. Beneath it stands the figure of St. Catherine of Siena, and hanging on the wall is the painting by Gérôme, Napoleon and the Sphinx.

The ceilings, windows, and painting of these octagonal bedrooms are entirely the work of modern craftsmen. The beds are sixteenth-century Florentine, and the drapes, gold silk with linen backing. The figure above the bed represents St. Anthony of Padua, who seems to protect the occupant as he slumbers. It is enameled terra cotta, the work of Andrea della Robbia, Italian, sixteenth century. The windows are tinted so that even on an overcast day the rooms appear to be sunny.

These octagonal tower bedrooms were the favorites of many VIPs including Winston Churchill, George Bernard Shaw, Arthur Brisbane, Hearst's chief editor, and even silent Cal Coolidge when he was President. Even though there are eighteen carillon bells in each tower above the bedrooms, no one complained about them, probably because there was something to deaden the sound: between the towers and the ceiling of each bedroom are huge water tanks each containing 2500 gallons used to service the Castle. If the bells didn't worry you, perhaps the 2500 gallons of water above would.

THE DOGE'S SUITE   Coming down the North Tower stairs we enter the living room of the Doge's Suite. It is on the second floor at the east side of the Castle, built directly over the Morning Room, and is named for the rulers of Venice in the days of the Venetian Republic. This is also known as the Blue Venetian Suite because the walls are completely covered with blue damask.

Over the sixteenth-century Italian fireplace is a bas-relief of the Virgin and Child by Giovanni della Robbia, and illuminated on either side are Italian metal candelabras. The shades on the large figure-based lamps, standing on the two early Venetian tables done in walnut, are alabaster and the floor is covered with a handsome blue Chinese rug.

One of the most striking features here is the rare ceiling, originally located in a Venetian building. Muraled and carved, it consists of two separate parts that were later combined into one ceiling. This is truly a magnificent room done in the opulence of the Baroque style of art—and the total atmosphere is of the grandeur of an era when Venice was mistress of the seas.

This was the suite favored by Millicent (Mrs. W.R.) Hearst when she visited San Simeon and served as the official hostess. This very rare snapshot shows Mrs. Hearst with her husband and five sons.

THE GAME ROOM   Returning to the first floor again, we are now in the Game Room, which was originally the breakfast room and much smaller. In the '30s Mr. Hearst had it converted into the billiard room, but these Brunswick tables were more for the guests than the host, as Mr. Hearst preferred the more active sports of swimming, tennis, and horseback riding.

Dominating this room is the oldest and rarest tapestry in the collection, a "Millefleur" hunt scene woven about five hundred years ago in Flanders, whose colors are hardly less brilliant today. The floor is covered with a mammoth Persian rug. Antique Persian tiles adorn the walls above the stone Byzantine archway. As we pass under this Romanesque arch you will see the console which on being opened reveals the keyboard used in playing the carillon bells in the towers.

Beyond that we will enter the Castle's private movie theatre where we will watch the première showing of Mr. Ken Murray's personal home movies of the early days here at San Simeon. This is to be a regular feature for tourists in the future, and starting today it will be the first time in history that any castle has been able to show actual motion pictures of the man who created it, living there and entertaining his friends.

Owning a collection of film is very much like owning a time machine. It enables one to relive an era that has long since vanished.

As I slipped out of the theatre before the film ended, walking toward La Casa del Mar, the only building closed to tourists, it occurred to me that San Simeon, like a collection of film, is also a kind of time machine which begins functioning for the visitor the moment he arrives. If he uses it properly and is observant, it will re-create for him the entire

time period and personal efforts which brought this unbelievable place into being.

I took the Esplanade, the wide walkway in a semicircle stretching around the Castle leading to the guesthouses, and was aware again that all of the landscaping and the subsidiary architecture were laid out in the same grand and imaginative scale as the Castle itself—and I thought of the interest Mr. Hearst must have had in the work of all of these skillful artisans who had made this possible.

I could see him as I never had before, poring over the plans of architect Julia Morgan, watching her sketch and resketch rooms with eager anticipation.

And then, in a much more homely way, his coming out of La Casa del Mar in the early days and walking about, fascinated by the craftsmen, bringing them lemonade, and encouraging them when the work was especially fine.

Having daily conferences with his lifelong friend, Nigel Keep, the patient horticulturist who devoted his entire life to the landscaping of the Enchanted Hill, a continuing transformation of the rocky hilltop into a vast garden of exotic beauty set among the carefully preserved oaks that Hearst loved.

Continuing, I marveled at the blending into the setting of the Hill's countless art objects. And the hundreds of feet of retaining walls and balustrades, necessary because of the different levels of the grounds, serving as ornamental backdrops for a profusion of marble statuary, Roman wellheads, sarcophagi, fountains, and ornate stairways and terraces.

I couldn't help but think of the enormous scope of his collection as I passed in front of one of the most impressive art works along the Esplanade—Sekhmet, the Egyptian goddess of war and destruction. This goes back to the eighteenth Egyptian dynasty and is the oldest item on the Hill. To form a more perfect setting a modern fountain was created backed by Roman columns, and the Egyptian theme was carried over even into the tile risers of the steps that lead to the main entrance in front of La Casa Grande. These interesting tiles were made in Spain. They are recognized as the finest of their kind. And I was able to think in some small way of Mr. Hearst—how he must have felt at first viewing this remarkable work of art before he had it disassembled, transported, and assembled again at San Simeon—and I had the feeling that his interest then was very deep and very vibrant in the work that some unknown artists or artisans had done all those centuries before in Egypt.

A bit farther along the Esplanade I came upon a grouping which illustrated perhaps more dramatically than any other at San Simeon the tremendous range of Mr. Hearst's interests. Here in this group—this one group—there is in the foreground a magnificent Greek sarcophagus, a burial vault. It was actually used as a chemical crematorium all that time ago, and it's very highly valued now because of its age, its rarity, and the remarkable carvings that go back to the second or third century before the birth of Christ. In the background there is a copy of Canova's *Three Graces*, the daughters of Zeus. This, of course, is a classical grouping in a classical theme but done in the Italian period. And then a curved bench, a balustrade, and columns that are modern Italian.

Flanking the approach to La Casa del Mar, Mr. Hearst's great love of animals is again illustrated by a magnificent three-hundred-year-old stylized Italian lion atop a pink limestone Verona marble fountain.

Reaching the entrance to La Casa del Mar, I found it the most unpretentious of all the guesthouses. The busts on pedestals on either side of the door have a special significance. They are Greek representing Alpha and Omega—meaning the beginning and the end—and it was here that Mr. Hearst's life at San Simeon began and ended.

At first glance, La Casa del Mar has the same look as the other guesthouses, characteristically Spanish with plain white wall surfaces, built on three levels with wide windows, doors, and cornices richly ornamented with stone. As in the other buildings, the Italian and

Spanish furnishings are harmoniously fused and the rooms are rich with magnificent carved gold-leaf columns, lovely Grecian urns, handsome statues, and exquisite paintings. One that particularly caught my eye was the work of the great Spaniard Goya, and I wondered if it could possibly be the one Bill Haines found on the back of that bathroom door in the Della Robbia Suite all those years ago.

Yes, on the surface this guesthouse seemed the same as the other buildings. But there was *one* difference. La Casa del Mar seemed to have a distinctly religious overtone. When you enter the vestibule the first thing you encounter is a beautiful statue of the Madonna and Child placed in an altarlike setting.

Mr. Hearst was a religious man, knew the Scriptures, and at one time possessed the best collection of Bibles in the world. The kind of art that pleased Hearst most was religious and medieval. His favorite subjects were youth and maternity, and his love of the Madonna is evident all over this domicile for the faces of Mother and Child gaze from tapestries, needlework, marble, terra cotta, glass, pottery, and oils.

Nominally an Episcopalian, he had always shown respect and tolerance for other forms of worship. He admired Christian Science, and regarded Gandhi as the greatest man of our century. Through the years he presented large gifts to Catholic Notre Dame University, Methodist-founded Northwestern University, and the Jewish Hospital in Denver, among many others.

I left La Casa del Mar by its back entrance—the one facing the Pacific—and stood for a moment on the wide loggia overlooking the blue sea. I leaned against the ancient columns that had been brought from Jerusalem and incorporated here. I wondered how many times Mr. Hearst had touched these columns of reddish purple porphyry and sensed the thousands of hands that through the centuries had worn them smooth.

Caught up and imbued with the excitement of the incredible past about me, I thought that perhaps the most remarkable thing of all about San Simeon was that it is still *alive*. Although its creator was gone in physical presence, something of his personality, his yearnings, and aspirations remain here. And perhaps the fullest illustration of that aliveness lay in the fact that magnificent as it is, San Simeon has never been finished.

I made my way back around the Castle to the back side of this over-whelming building, and there I saw on either hand evidence of the incomplete nature of this greatest of all dwelling places. There was more work to be done here and certainly a plan for these endeavors was somewhere inside the mind of William Randolph Hearst. But when the Chief left San Simeon for the last time in 1947 he was eighty-four years old and in failing health—he would never see his lifelong dream finished, and we never will either.

If William Randolph Hearst were still alive he would still be build-ing. But time ran out—as it must for us all.

AUTHOR'S NOTE

The compilation of a book of this nature presents unimaginable difficulties and cannot be accomplished singlehandedly. Although I have built up my own collection of Hearstiana for over three decades, the historical section of this book is in greatest measure its contribution, and the cooperation and generosity of many individuals and institutions were necessary from its commencement to completion.

Of all acknowledgments and debts of thanks due and owing, the principal one must go to Wes Cater and his staff at the California State Historical Monument—San Simeon. Locating and identifying the valuable collection of historical photographs, documents, and drawings of upwards of five thousand negatives, with the assistance of Mrs. Irene Hanks and a former Hearst employee, Mrs. Ann Rotanzi, who is still at the Castle, was the source principally relied on by the author for the graphic presentation of San Simeon history, every example of which is authentic.

Special and permanent reference is also due here to Dick Thompson, Information Officer of the Department of Parks and Recreation for the State of California, and to the following individuals: Gerald Reynolds, Metta Hake, James Evans, Charles de Vogel, and Bill Atkinson, who helped me search the archives located in the deep, dark reaches in the basement of San Simeon for historical material.

Grateful acknowledgment is also made to the many friends—Sybil and Harry Brand, Bill Haines, Loretta Young, Pat Lake, Mary Brian, Claire Windsor, King Vidor, Eileen Percy, Turnley Walker, Billy Bakewell, Miss Lee Wenzlick, Jimmy Shields, Howard Strickling, and Cary Grant—for their anecdotes and reminiscences of the days and nights on the Enchanted Hill.

Last, but certainly not least, my long-time friend Arthur Lake, whose enthusiasm that I "must meet the Chief" made this whole project possible.

To all of the above, I am their debtor for help, which I could not only never repay, but don't even know how to give thanks.

KEN MURRAY
Beverly Hills, California

INDEX